Villains and Vi

The Global Drug, Terrorism Crime Conund

By Robert Tennant-Ralphs

Drug policies adopted by governments, and treatments offered for addiction, pain and mental problems by the medical world combine in a relationship to negatively affects the world's most vulnerable people. *Villains and Victims. The Global Drug, Terrorism and Organised Crime Conundrum* exposes how this unchallenged negative symbiosis influences the human world: seemingly unrelated policies act symbiotically to increase addiction, organised crime, radicalisation, and ultimately terrorism. At first, it was an unintended chain, but the evidence suggests much of it is now deliberate. The public needs to be made aware of the harm the policies are causing.

For over a hundred years, the knock-on effect of the world's ineffective drug laws and drug substitution policies contributed to the deaths of millions of people. Unless the regimes that cause this are changed, governments will continue to misguide us, pharmaceutical firms make huge unethical profits, and doctors will not offer the best treatments for drug addiction and alcoholism. This means millions more men, women, and children will continue to suffer and die from their effects, as well as from terrorist attacks and organised crime.

1

Contents

Preface - The Moroccan Conundrum.
Dedication
Forward
Introduction

Part 1 - Terrorism.

Chapter 1   Casablanca bombings 2003.
Chapter 2   Effects and causes of Morocco's drug issues.
Chapter 3   Total Abstinence vs Harm Reduction.
Chapter 4   Madrid bombings 2004.
Chapter 5   London terrorist attacks 2005 and 2017.
Chapter 6   Marrakech bombing 2011.
Chapter 7   Paris terrorist attacks 2015.
Chapter 8   Brussels terrorist attacks 2016.
Chapter 9   Barcelona terrorist attacks 2017
Chapter 10 9/11 and the Iraq war.

Part 2

Chapter 11 Organised crime in the Netherlands and Belgium.
Chapter 12 Solution to Global Drug Problems.

Epilogue.

The contents include photographs of the devastation caused by terrorist attacks and organised crime, memorial plaques, and some of those sites today. Interviews with survivors and families affected. Explanations of good and bad drug policies, and the best treatment for drug addiction and alcoholism based on global experience.

Preface

The Moroccan Conundrum.

At the 2022 football World Cup, the Dr Jekyll character of Morocco's football team won the hearts of millions of underdog lovers, but there are Moroccans whose character is more like the murderous Mr. Hyde.

At the same time their footballers applied their skills at the Dubai World Cup, in Brussels and Amsterdam, court cases were taking place that charged some of their countrymen with two of the worst crimes of the 21ˢᵗ century. If, as expected, the men on trial are found guilty, they will spend the rest of their lives in prison.

Although each crime was despicable, because the Belgian and Dutch cases were for offences in different countries, the juries are unlikely to be made aware of an important fact. The acts of deadly terrorism in Brussels in 2016, and the organised crime murder in Amsterdam in 2021, for which the suspects are being tried are connected. This means the factors that lead Moroccans to continually commit such atrocities will not be addressed. As these include the Barcelona, Brussels, Paris, London, Madrid, Marrakesh, Casablanca and 9/11 terrorist attacks, 14 murders by the Moroccan mafia in the Netherlands, and 1,659 Moroccans joining ISIS this century, it is essential they are corrected.

To put in place the policies that will prevent them the reasons need to be understood. Whereas, putting yesteryear's culprits behind bars is not the answer. That will not prevent other Moroccans, or people from different countries, for the same reasons, from committing such crimes in the years ahead.

But are the criminals who commit terrorist attacks and organised crime the only *villains*? Or is this book right, as it suggests, there are others less visibly responsible, such as politicians, pharmaceutical firms, and medical professionals?

We know who the *victims* are. They suffer as the direct result of other people's actions and inactions. We owe it to them to do everything we can to correct the situation.

****

Villains and Victims. The Global Drug, Terrorism and Organised Crime Conundrum author explains that he believes the causes of many of the world's drug problems are the result of global drug laws and policies, misinformation by pharmaceutical firms, and politicians with dubious agendas.

Knowing this, clears the way to understand the root causes and then apply effective solutions.

****

From the top of a mountain in May 2017, I looked down into a valley where cannabis grew under a bright yellow sun. I looked up and watched clouds float by. I realised I understood only a little about life in Morocco's Rif mountains and the reasons why the infamous plant grown here caused many problems.
I closed my eyes; very soon I began to understand.

Morocco's hypocritical drug laws and misguided addiction treatment policies, and America's delusional war on drugs were much to blame for Moroccans' involvement in Europe's worst terrorist attacks and influence on organised crime.

After walking a little way down, I stopped, wondering if there was more I needed to understand. I closed my eyes again. This time words from the Qur'an entered my mind, 'Take a life and it is as though you took the lives of all mankind. Save a life and it as if you saved all humanity.'
I understood all I needed to know.

The Bush Administration, Tony Blair and José María Aznar leading the USA, UK and Spain into the Iraq war; Donald Trump and Boris Johnson's Islamophobic acts or words; the pharmaceutical industry misleading doctors about the best treatment for addiction; King Mohamed VIth' s life of luxury while millions of Moroccans are uneducated and live in poverty, also played significant roles.

So began my search for a solution. As I found only evidence of Morocco applying ineffective ways to address these issues, and none that put in place the best policies to stop them, I wondered what prevented this?

- Are King Mohammed VIth and Morocco's government aware what the best policies are?
- Are they afraid to investigate the problems, thinking it could open a can of worms and cause a public backlash at home and globally?
- Do they know there are policies and regimes that work in other countries that would fix many of their drug problems?

But there was one question that would be unknown to most people that also needed answering,

- Why are there more recovered Moroccan drug addicts living in each of France, Spain, Belgium, the Netherlands, the UK, and the USA than the whole of Morocco? If I could answer that, maybe it would be the key to addressing all of Morocco's drug issues. Many of which are the same problems globally.

Dedication

Villains and Victims. The Global Drug, Terrorism and Organised Crime Conundrum is dedicated to the families of every man, woman and child killed or injured in this century's terrorist attacks in Casablanca, Madrid, London, Paris, Marrakesh, Brussels, Barcelona, and the USA. Thousands died, tens of thousands were injured, witnesses to the atrocities from ambulance, fire, hospital, and police services suffered post-traumatic stress, while families, friends and communities will still feel the consequences for years to come.

Villains and Victims. The Global Drug, Terrorism and Organised Crime Conundrum is also dedicated to those who suffer the consequences of Moroccan organised crime mafias who traffic drugs through the Netherlands, Belgium, Spain, France, Italy, and Portugal to the rest of Europe.

Villains and Victims. The Global Drug, Terrorism and Organised Crime Conundrum in addition is dedicated to the millions of drug addicts and alcoholics in the world. They end up in hospitals, prisons or dead, while their families suffer heartache as they watch loved ones slowly destroy themselves.

Forward

Eulogio Paz President of the Asociación 11-M Affectados del Terrorismo (Victims Affected by Terrorism) and father of Daniel who was killed along with 191 others in the 2004 Madrid bombings.

On the morning of 11ᵗʰ March 2004, I was at my workplace when the phone on a colleague's table rang. Upon answering, a woman asked me if Miguel had arrived; I told her that he hadn't. "Some bombs have exploded at the Estación de Atocha, and I don't know if something could have happened to him", she replied. I quickly went online, checked the route of the trains and where the bombs had exploded.

Then, I called Pilar, our son Daniel's mother. I asked what news she had. She answered, crying, that she had been trying to get in touch with him. I remember a phrase she used in between the tears: "I want to die."

Then, I called Daniel's mobile phone, but he didn't answer. I sent a message saying, "call me". I was slow to react.

At about ten o'clock that morning, my company arranged a car for me to go and search for Daniel. I went to different hospitals, ending at the Institución Ferial de Madrid (IFEMA) trade exhibition centre where they were providing updates. We were there all that day and night.

After the DNA tests that were carried out on Pilar and me, they told us that we could leave. They would let us know if they had any news.

They notified us *five days later*, on March 16 2004, to pick up Daniel's body. We took him to a funeral home where we watched over him. He was cremated the next day, on March 17th.

About ten days after Daniel's vile murder, I went to the *El Pozo* train station. His absence took me to the places whose surroundings he was perhaps last able to see, while the train carrying him suddenly stopped and ended his life.

It was the possibility of finding words left by his friends that took me to the *El Pozo* station. In the tower at the Cercanías commuter train station, there were candles, flowers, and messages written on the ground, on sheets of paper, and on the red iron tubes. I read them as best I could, and without going to the platform, I walked through the passageway that, under the tracks, connects one side to the other of the station. Here there were more flowers, candles, black ribbons, writings, photos, and drawings dedicated to those murdered, covering walls and glass.

The day was cloudy, like my eyes. A feeling of disbelief and emptiness enveloped my steps when I left the station.

With the passing of the days, I thought that the weather (physical and meteorological) and cleaning services would eventually erase the words, messages, and writings. I did not want them to be lost, to be forgotten. I thought of going back to copy them. I went there on a sunny Sunday afternoon in April. I wrote down in an old white notebook with blue stripes the sentences I could read. I stayed for a while, writing, imagining, watching...

Seeing people walking by,
people watching,
people stopping.
Watching life pass by,
memories and sleeplessness,
illusions and joys.
Seeing lost loves go by.
Watching the trains pass by,
echoing down the tracks.
red and white trains,
Cercanías trains.
trains of suffering,
trains with melancholic messages,
arriving trains,
departing trains.
Trains. Those trains.
The trains of that day...

During the trial held over four months in 2007, I requested life imprisonment for Daniel's murderers. I also claimed there was a political responsibility hanging over those who governed at the time. I recalled something I had said days before March 11th, 2004, the sort of comment you make when talking to friends, relatives, and acquaintances.

"Here, someday, on account of the photo taken in the Azores of Blair, Bush, Aznor and the Portuguese leader, they are going to hit us with a *pepinazo* (terror attack)".

I went back to work eleven days after Daniel's murder. I had two options, to stay in bed, staring at the ceiling or get up and walk. I got up and walked, I started trying to find reasons why Daniel was killed, and follow the intuition I had, "they are going to hit us with a *pepinazo* on account of the Azores photo".

By reading different newspapers, I found something that caught my attention. The Fundación para el Análisis y los Estudios Sociales - FAES (The People's Party think-tank) said at the beginning of 2003, that is before the attacks - I remember because it had stuck with me -, "it is expected there will be an intensification of terrorist threats if there is a war against Iraq, a threat that will affect the countries that intervene".

Did FAES, the foundation of José María Aznar, president of the Government of the Popular Party that governed Spain on March 11, 2004, anticipate he would lead Spain into joining the USA and UK in attacking Iraq, and what would happen as a result?

In June 2016, twelve years after the attacks, the members of the Asociación 11-M Affectados del Terrorismo agreed that I should be the new president. Since then, I have tried to contribute to the well-being of the victims of terrorism by obtaining medical aid for the injured, and relatives of the injured and deceased, which includes psychological, social assistance, training, and legal aid. These fundamental tasks undertaken by our association would fall short if we did not also address awareness and education, to prevent people in the future from suffering from the effects of terrorism.

Our exhibition "Trazos y puntadas para el recuerdo" '(Strokes and Stitches to Remember)', our magazine *11MAGINA*, coexistence activities, conferences and debates, contribute to this task.

Also very important is the construction of a narrative, that condemning without palliatives terrorism, explains but does not justify the different origins of it. Only then may it be possible to come to understand and remedy the root causes.

Also important is to preserve an accurate account of what happened that leads to the individual and collective memory and ensures that the victims of terrorism are not forgotten and remain in the memory of humanity.

For this, services In Memoriam, the respect and care of monuments and memorial spaces are a duty of institutions and guarantors of justice and dialogue between different entities, so that the intolerance and economic, political and religious fundamentalisms (hotbeds for terrorism) that exist are prevented from causing the derailment of our society.

****

Xavier Albiac son of one the victims of the Casablanca terrorist attack that killed 33 people and injured more than 100 in 2003.

My name is Xavier Albiac Cruxent. I was born in 1974. I am the youngest son of three brothers. Manuel, Monica and me. My parents are Manuel and Pilar. My family are Catalan industrialists on both my mother's and father's sides.

On May 16, 2003, my father was assassinated in a terrorist attack in Casablanca, Morocco. He was 58 years old. It destroyed the lives of all the people who loved, respected or had friendship with my father. Time heals wounds, but scars remain forever.

His mother died 13 days before this happened, so luckily, she did not suffer from it. Whereas my grandfather lost his son, my uncle lost his brother, my cousins lost their uncle, my mother lost her beloved husband and Manolo, Monica and I lost our beloved father. While many people lost a friend and employer. We could not say goodbye to him.

Manuel Albiac
Cruxent

Manuel's wife

Someone made this happen. We were told few facts, some truths, some lies, behind his and the deaths of all the victims.

We as ordinary citizens, live different ways of life depending on our country's culture, education, or religion. But we all try to live in the best possible way and in peace. In a democratic society, people are free and can decide for themselves.

However, there are rulers who are not interested in the education of the people because they know that if their citizens are educated, they will be difficult to dominate. At the same time, many rulers take advantage of their power or their voice to manipulate and lie. Examples were the manipulative presidents: Bush, Blair and Aznar when they talked about weapons prior to the Iraq War.

So, I ask, why is my father not with us now? Is he not among us because some poor wretches were deceived by being told that if you kill for God, you will reach paradise? Or is he not among us because there are people who took advantage of their situation to lie, create hatred and make these events take place?

I know who I would forgive and who I will never forgive. I know that even though he can't enjoy it, my father is by my side. Every day I say, 'Thanks dad, for giving me life. I am sorry you are not here to enjoy it with me.'

Today is for Peace
Commemorative picture in Xavier Albiac's, Pigal Hotel, Tarragona

11

Introduction

Villains and Victims. The Global Drug, Terrorism and Organised Crime Conundrum exposes the reasons behind these criminal acts, and others in Europe and the USA, by revealing how governments, pharmaceutical firms, the police, and medical professionals do not address the reasons effectively. Which in some instances, seems to have even been done deliberately.

A retrospective examination shows how Moroccans were the 21st century's leading perpetrators of most of Europe's worst crimes.

With major court cases involving Moroccan terrorists and murderers taking place in Brussels and Amsterdam at the same time in 2022 and 2023, it could have put the spotlight on why it is invariably Moroccans. But unfortunately, it did not.

However, analysis of the facts makes clear that much of the blame lies elsewhere. It shows that almost every country has influenced it, and each should look at how their policies continue to contribute to the problems. After that, hopefully, they too would apply regimes that are known to work.

Sadly, the lack of understanding of the causes and solutions to drug-related problems are at the highest levels in some of the world's leading law and policy-making advisory organisations. This was evidenced in March 2022 when the United Nations Office on Drugs and Crime (UNODC) hosted a workshop in Rabat to help Morocco with its problems. The following is the UNODC's published summary of the workshop.

'In recent years, Morocco has developed a comprehensive rule of law-based counter-terrorism strategy, which includes robust security measures, regional and international cooperation, and terrorist counter-radicalization policies. Still, foreign terrorist fighters (FTFs) who fled their countries to join the ranks of ISIL/Da'esh and other terrorist groups are returning to their homes and pose severe security threats.

It is estimated that over 1,600 Moroccans have migrated to Iraq and Syria since 2013. Among them, government officials say there are close to 300 women and more than 620 children and minors.

To respond to this imminent security challenge, UNODC delivered a workshop in Rabat to support Morocco build capacity to investigate terrorist offences, including FTFs and returnees (RFTFs), in accordance with the rule of law, human rights, and gender dimensions considerations on 28-30 March 2022.

The event brought together 21 Moroccan criminal justice and law enforcement officials from the Ministries of Interior and Justice, and the Superior Council of the Judiciary. National and international experts from the UN Analytical Support and Monitoring Team of the ISIL/Da'esh and Al-Qaida Sanctions Committee, UNODC, the Spanish National Police, the Moroccan Faculty of Law Mohammedia, the Deputy Public Prosecutor of the King at the Court of Appeal in Rabat all contributed with their in-depth expertise.

The event built the expertise of Moroccan stakeholders in developing effective and human rights-compliant investigation and trial management standards for RFTFs, including youth, women, and family members associated with terrorist groups.

Moreover, current national and regional developments and threats associated with RFTFs and their family members were addressed, as well as the challenges and good practices in international cooperation. One participant recalled that "without international collaboration, there can be no effective counter-terrorism strategy." Case studies illustrated the successful counter-terrorism cooperation between Spain and Morocco and their good practices in cooperating in terrorist investigations.'

Although, its purpose was well intentioned the workshop lacked the background knowledge essential to deliver its objective, therefore it only dealt with a small part of the problem. It did not address the underlying reasons why so many Moroccans become terrorists or go into organised crime. Nor how to prevent more of their citizens doing the same in future. It only dealt with ways which may help those already radicalised, although there is no certainty that would be achieved. While the comment, *"without international collaboration, there can be no effective counter-terrorism strategy"* is accurate and what is needed.

Villains and Victims. The Global Drug, Terrorism and Organised Crime Conundrum clarifies the reasons and puts forward a workable solution.

As it was deeply embedded preventable reasons that caused 1,659 Moroccans to join ISIS, and many more to be involved in terrorist attacks, it is essential to expose what those reasons are. Only then will the remedies for the underlying issues caused by the self-centered interests and motives of the ruling class be put in place. Doing this should not only remove the bad policies that created the situation but would also have a positive effect on Moroccan society. With the knock-on benefits transcending Europe and beyond.

Today I vacillate between deep sadness each time I see solvent sniffing drug-addicted street children and extreme frustration when I consider the unaccountability of Morocco's political regime that won't help its people.

Whereas, if Morocco acts now, it could put in motion policies that would stop it from being the worst of the baddies and put it on a path to be the best of goodies.

To do that it needs help on two external fronts.

a.   The pharmaceutical industry needs to tell Morocco's medical profession that the way they *exclusively* use drug substitution to deal with addiction and alcoholism is wrong: these are *diseases,* and this policy will never work to remedy the underlying causes.

b.   Morocco's government must appoint an external non-affiliated group of experts from countries with the most successful drug laws and positive results from addiction treatment to advise them. The aim being to replace each of their bad policies with those that are good.

In terms of the number of people killed and its spectacular imagery, the terrorist attack on the World Trade Centre in New York, known as 9/11, was the most horrific in history. However, terrorist attacks in Spain, France, Belgium, United Kingdom, and Morocco this century have also had horrendous consequences.

When looked at collectively, we see the overall effect and widespread influence of terrorism, though we can also see that most of the terrorists were of Moroccan origin. On three continents, in six countries, in a dozen cities, at twenty-five locations, radicalised men and women committed some of the worst ever crimes imaginable. Thousands of men, women, and children died, while thousands more were injured, families and communities suffered, and those alive still suffer.

As the reason why it was so often Moroccans has never been properly addressed by the authorities and police, the likelihood is there will be more. And as the past attacks were indiscriminate and the diaspora of Moroccans is widespread, few places or sects of people are safe.

Part 1 of *Villains and Victims. The Global Drug, Terrorism and Organised Crime Conundrum* clarifies previously overlooked factual evidence that causes people to be radicalised into committing terrorist attacks, especially Moroccans. By not analysing at sufficient depth the underlying reasons, the actions of the authorities and police to date, have not and will never work. As closer examination reveals that solutions are possible, it is important to put these in place as soon as possible before there are more attacks.

Part 2 of *Villains or Victims? The Global Drug, Terrorism and Organised Crime Conundrum.* For the past 100 years, the consequences of organised crime globally have been devastating. Italian, Russian, American, Mexican, Israeli, Albanian, Columbian, Serbian mafias, Chinese triads, the Japanese Yakuza, and other such groups, have wreaked havoc on people and communities wherever such criminal organisations exist. In more recent years, the same is true of the Moroccan 'Mocro-Maffia' in the Netherlands and Belgium. But as the reasons for this are identifiable and correctable, putting together a proposal to eradicate them should be high on the agenda of the Moroccan, Dutch, and Belgian authorities. Unfortunately, in the spring of 2023, this is not the case, only temporary fixes are being applied.

Villains and Victims. The Global Drug, Terrorism and Organised Crime Conundrum explains the background of the perpetrators - who are not all classified as criminals as they include politicians, businessmen, and medical professionals - followed by factual evidence which, when exposed, clarifies what needs to be done to initiate workable solutions.

Part 1

Terrorism and Organised Crime

The majority of those who committed the worst terrorist attacks in Europe this century were of Moroccan origin. In addition, over 1,650 Moroccans joined the terrorist group, ISIS, while Moroccans are responsible for much of Europe's organised crime. But none of these men and women were born terrorists or criminals, so what made them that way?

As the perpetrators or their criminal activities often have links to illegal drugs, politicians applied laws and policies that have not worked. As the content in *Villains and Victims. The Global Drug, Terrorism and Organised Crime Conundrum,* explains, although those in authority in Morocco condemn the criminal acts of its citizens, very little of the best remedial action is in place to prevent them. This is because the root causes are not addressed; its law makers' perennial failings, while their medical professionals do not administer the best drug addiction treatment.

Although the direct perpetrators of 9/11 and Europe's 20th century terrorist attacks are behind bars or dead, and rightly branded as terrorists and criminals, there are people less obviously responsible, who carry on with their lives as if they are blameless.

At the same time, the mothers, fathers, husbands, wives, sons and daughters of the **victims** and communities where they lived, still suffer because of their actions or inactions.

To prevent more attacks and to minimise organised crime, *Villains and Victims. The Global Drug, Terrorism and Organised Crime Conundrum* exposes who they are, what they did, or did not do, and what needs to be done to remedy this situation.

****

Every country has drug problems. They range from accidents, sickness, death and family disfunction to radicalisation into terrorism and organised crime. Many are the result of governments' wrong doings and hypocritical drug laws. The medical profession not applying the best treatment for addiction, and the misleading claims of pharmaceutical firms based on greed.

As there are established solutions that would fix many of these issues, plus save millions of lives and mountains of money, *Villains and Victims. The Global Drug, Terrorism and Organised Crime Conundrum,* asks why are they not applied everywhere?

In the instants of time, the bad experience of this past century's drug policies holds the keys to successfully deal with all the world's drug problems, especially their appalling criminal consequences and addiction. The problem is, at this time in 2023, only a small percentage of the world's population understands this. While many in business prevent it happening by exploiting the situation for personal gain and politicians for fear of public backlash.

Villains and Victims. The Global Drug, Terrorism and Organised Crime Conundrum is based on facts. Its content explains how there are solutions to these issues that work when they are applied. By first outlining the background, the reasons, effect, and consequences of the world's past bad drug practices, it then provides evidence of the positive results in countries where better policies are applied. In conclusion, this book puts forward workable solutions and innovative extensions of these.

****

By the time the I went to live in Morocco in January 2017, to help its 1,200,000 drug addicts and alcoholics, I had accumulated much experience regarding drugs, addiction, and recovery. As a result, I quickly understood how difficult this would be when I realised how using cannabis - like alcohol in non-Muslim countries - is a way of life in Morocco, and trafficking it along with other drugs, finances many Moroccan's livelihoods, there, and in Europe.

What I also learned in the next few years, was that this had a huge societal cost in Europe, as it included radicalisation into terrorism, and financed organised crime. While in Morocco itself, the country's drug laws I came to realise are farcical, and its medical profession gives the wrong treatment to drug addicts and alcoholics. In fact, what they all too often do makes them worse!

I am qualified to say this for several reasons. For twenty-five years I was a practicing drug addict and alcoholic. In 1985 I quit all mood-altering substances and have been abstinent ever since, now 38 years.

For over thirty years I have helped drug addicts and alcoholics recover and witnessed hundreds of thousands do the same who applied 12-Step recovery programmes. As these are working in 175 countries in 80 languages and have enabled over 3,500,000 to recover their success cannot be disputed.

My experience also includes 35 years as a management consultant and business development adviser to the pharmaceutical industry. Though I began my working life in the British police where I studied drug laws.

To do research for this book and a documentary series, in 2022 I visited the sites of the Barcelona, Cambrils and Madrid terrorist attacks. I also spent six days in Ripoll, the hometown of the ten Moroccan terrorists responsible for the Barcelona attack, and Alcanar, near Tarragona where they had their bomb making factory.

I already knew the explosives used in the Madrid attacks were paid for by Moroccan drugs; now I wondered if there were links to drugs associated with the Barcelona attacks?

After talking too young people, including Moroccans, living in Ripoll, I found out about the widespread use of drugs by those who lived there. From this I concluded that the convicted Moroccan drug trafficker, Abdelbaki Es Satty, then claiming to be an imam, used drugs to influence the Moroccan terrorists living in Ripoll that he radicalised.

But, if that was true, why was it not in the official report or recently made documentary series about the attack?

After talking to Ripoll police officers and others in the Catalan region who knew the background, pooling all I found out with my experience, gave me an answer. The subject of drugs could have been taboo as dealing in them had been going on under the noses of the police.

In 2004 Es Satty was given a three-year prison sentence for trying to smuggle 120 kilograms of cannabis into Ceuta, the Spanish enclave in north Morocco near its Rif Mountain cannabis growing region. To do a deal of this size, he must have had well established contacts on both shores of the Mediterranean, growers in Morocco and drug dealers in Spain.

As this amount of cannabis was worth $500,000 at street value, the people Es Satty was trafficking it for were big time drug dealers; that amount of cannabis would never be a one-off. This meant he must have had drug trafficking experience before he was caught and was big time as well.

As a Moroccan and a dealer, Es Satty would have known the effects of taking cannabis, especially how it loosens the mind. As statistically many people are potential addicts, at least one of the terrorists probably would have been, so he would have been particularly easy to manipulate, addicts will do anything to get drugs, including dyeing for them. And as all the terrorists were young Moroccans who are renowned for trying to live in a macho world, it would be absurd to think they had not abused cannabis.

Invariably too, cannabis would have been in their backgrounds. Their origins were north Moroccon, where the aroma of cannabis in cafes is thick in the air. Tangier's Café Hafa and Café Baba are on the cannabis seeking tourist agenda. The likes of Bob Marley and the Rolling Stones made sure of that.

In his book, *'Horses of God'* about the Casablanca terrorist attacks in 2003, the author, Mahi Binebine makes clear how drugs were part of the imam who orchestrated that attacks radicalisation programme.

Equally relevant to Morocco's horrendous background regarding drugs is the effect of Karkoubi, a cocktail of solvent, cannabis and benzodiazapine - usually Rivotril made by Roche - which is taken with alcohol.

Karkoubi is exclusive to Morocco and not called, 'the drug of mass destruction' and 'drug of the poor' for nothing, it is cheap and makes its abusers feel all-powerful, and has influenced some to go on killing sprees.

To complete his research, the author interviewed the families of victims of terrorist attacks and organised crime, police officers in Europe's drug trafficking hot spots - Amsterdam and Antwerp - Moroccan doctors, psychiatrists, pharmacists, cannabis growers in the Rif Mountains, drug dealers, a Mena Region's

18

leading political analyst and a Brussels MEP. He also met recovered drug addicts and alcoholics who shared their experiences in thirty-four countries.

But sadly, as there is only a handful of Moroccans in recovery living in the whole country, this was not helpful to Morocco. Whereas attending AA and NA meetings in London, Paris, Madrid, Barcelona, Amsterdam, Brussels, New York and Lisbon was most enlightening because I met recovered Moroccan drug addicts and alcoholics living in each.

These experiences introduced an interesting concept to my better understanding of the situation.

It is estimated by the WHO that approximately 5% of the world population has an addiction problem. The population of Morocco is approximately 35,000,000. Their diaspora of over 5,000,000, mostly spread across Europe and North America, means there are some 40,000,000 Moroccans globally.

Based on these figures, living in Morocco are approximately 1,750,000 addicts and 250,000 in other countries. As there are so few who are recovered in Morocco, while there are many in other countries, it is clear something is wrong with Morocco's internal policies.

Putting all I knew together; I identified common factors with regard to the reasons for terrorism and organised crime.

These include biased, misinformed, political manipulation, corruption, hypocritical drug laws, ineffective treatment of addiction, not treating addiction as a disease, pharmaceutical firms miss-selling, ignorance and poverty.

It was all this which helped me understand why there have been so many Moroccans involved in terrorist attacks in Europe, Morocco, and America's 9/11.

****

If instead of spending €11 billion on defence (or attack), Morocco spent it on drug addiction treatment, rehabilitation, and wiping out poverty, it would make the world and Morocco a better and safer place.

Although it seems by some of his actions King Mohamed VIth tries to help, other actions and inactions do the opposite. His lifestyle of spending €'s billions on palaces, luxury cars, and €1 million watches, carries a distinct message. Whereas spending it on citizens who live in poverty would carry a far more beneficial one.

An issue that doesn't help Morocco's international reputation is its lack of freedom of the press. With the rank of 1 as good, Morocco's of 136 out of 170 countries by Reporters Without Borders puts it in the bottom quarter on their global list.

As its approach is used to silence journalists, it automatically raised the question of why? As I came to understand more about Morocco, I also came to an obvious conclusion.

Over five million Moroccans now live abroad. They chose their new country because they believed there would be a better life there for them and their children. In most instances, their diaspora took them to Europe or North America.

One of the greatest benefits in their new countries is to a family's females. In Morocco girls and women are treated as inferior by boys and men, which means many are frequently physically abused. This often includes rape, many of which are unreported for fear of repercussions, plus there is the stigma that goes with being a rape victim: a stigma that can last for the victim's lifetime.

On 29th March 2023 a rape case in Morocco caused shock and outrage at the leniency of the judge's sentencing. Three men who repeatedly raped an 11-year-old girl and made her pregnant were sentenced to two years in prison plus nominal fines. They also threatened to kill her family if she reported it.

If this happened in the Western countries where the Moroccans moved to, each rapist would have received a sentence ranging from 10 years to life in prison.

Those in power in Morocco want to avoid the exposure of issues like this as much as possible and the best way they know to do that is to silence journalists. But continually turning a blind eye to the fact the world is moving towards press freedom, means such actions speak ever more loudly. And Moroccans living abroad know the reality, which can only have a demoralising effect.

But hiding what they do, or admitting what they have done when it is wrong, seems to be part of many Moroccans' psyche or DNA.

Each European city where Moroccan-led terrorist attacks took place commemorates them annually with services of remembrance for those who died: while in Casablanca and Marrakech, this is low-key with regard to the Europeans killed by its terrorists. And has Morocco's king or government apologised to the families of the victims or offered compensation? This would show it took some responsibility for its countrymen's wrongdoings.

In 2003 in Casablanca eight Europeans were killed, in 2011 in Marrakesh thirteen died, in 2018 there another tragedy in Morocco shocked the world. Two young female Scandinavian tourists were brutally beheaded in the High Atlas Mountains, near a famed beauty spot, Mount Toubkal. The killers were young uneducated Moroccans from poor families and frequently influenced by drugs.

Village of Imil in the Atlas Mountains site of the Scandinavian girl's murders.
A Morocco World News article, part of which is published in the USA, showed a good understanding of the situation.

"Morocco should address the conditions conducive to the emergence and spread of terrorism by fighting poverty and social disparity in the country... promoting the culture of peace and coexistence through education... ensuring humans rights ...and promoting the universal values of peace, justice, co-existence, integrity, love, and cross-cultural dialogue..."

After two years living in Morocco and six years helping its drug addicts, I visited the sites of the major terrorist attacks and cities with the worst organised crime in Europe. This convinced me that nothing had been done which would significantly change Morocco's deep-rooted drug problems and their consequences. My mission in life since has been to do all I could to prevent more attacks.

By writing *Villains or Victims, A Global Drug and Terrorism Conundrum,* and making a documentary series of the contents, I hope will play a part in achieving this. *Inshallah*

Chapter 1

Casablanca Bombings 2003.

I had reached the point in life where I seldom listened to news programmes or read newspapers; they invariably contained the same gloom and doom items I had heard or read about daily for over fifty years. But, at 9 am on Friday 16th May 2003, I turned my radio on to hear the weather forecast; I had a tennis match organised for later that morning.

The first item said that the previous night a series of bomb attacks had killed thirty-three innocent people in Casablanca; and more than a hundred were injured. Later news reported that the attacks were carried out by fourteen suicide bombers who also died.

The attacks that occurred were a series of coordinated strikes at a Spanish restaurant, the Belgian consulate, a Jewish community centre, and the 5* Farah Maghreb Hotel.

España Club Terrorist Attack, Casablanca 2003

Jewish Community Centre, Casablanca 2003

The terrorists came from Sidi Moumen, an extremely poor suburb of Casablanca. Yachine was one of the main perpetrators. He and his ten brothers grew up there. To escape their daily surroundings and lifestyles, from an early age they took drugs, they also started a football team - *Les Etoiles de Sidi Moumen* - the Stars of Sidi Moumen.

With Morocco's national men's team known as the 'Lions of the Atlas' being world-class, they dreamed of playing for it one day. But that dream changed when Yachine's older brother Hamid began attending religious meetings with Sheikh Abou Zoubeir. Within a matter of weeks, Zoubeir had persuaded the Stars of Sidi Moumen to believe there was a better world in the afterlife, where their faith in Allah would be rewarded. They needed only to choose between dying gloriously or living disgracefully. For Yachine and the Stars of Sidi Moumen this was a no-brainer. The choice was obvious.

A few years earlier, I had visited Casablanca on business. Now, as I sat in my Notting Hill home in London taking in this horrific news and images, little did I realise this attack would be one of a series of similar incidents that would change the direction of my life forever. My understanding of the reasons for them meant I would embark upon a journey that would lead me to try to prevent similar Moroccan-influenced terrorist attacks.

Although I had been a regular visitor to Morocco, I was now 58 and knew little about its links to drugs, organised crime, and terrorism. Today, I know more about these subjects than most people on the planet.

This may seem like an arrogant statement, but it is based on fact and personal experience. Whereas the politicians and legal advisors who make drug laws and doctors who decide treatment policies in Morocco do so based on theory, self-interest, and lack first-hand knowledge.

As knowledge of these is essential to understand Morocco's many complex drug problems, it is not surprising its drug-related issues are horrendous. You would not let an unqualified surgeon remove a cancer tumour or perform a heart transplant, but this is the case regarding drug laws and policies in Morocco.

Aged fifteen I was introduced to alcohol and cigarettes. I liked their effect so much that in the next twenty-five years, I developed a relationship with them and other drugs - *especially prescription* - from which I nearly died. During this time, I went from being a social drinker and casual drug user to an out-of-work drug-addicted criminal.

Soon after I quit all drugs in 1985, I returned to my earlier profession as a business development adviser to the pharmaceutical industry; a position I have had ever since. As my international client base grew, I travelled to many countries, and because of my recovery from drug addiction and alcoholism, I tried to help drug addicts and alcoholics in each country I visited. In all but one, I had some success; that exception was Morocco.

Another influence I had was as a serving British police officer. It was the 1960's and the hippie culture of smoking cannabis and flower power was all the rage. I sat on the fence of the law I was supposed to uphold on one side, and as a cannabis user from which I got pleasure, I sat on the other.

This combination of experiences meant I had spent twenty-five years learning what is bad about the effect of mood-altering addictive drugs. Conversely, for the next thirty-seven, I focussed on doing what I could to help drug addicts and their families.

But why Morocco? What was different about it? I kept wondering, so I went to live there to find out.

When I moved to Tangier at the end of 2016, I had only one agenda; to help drug addicts, alcoholics, and their families. As time passed, I learned more about the difficulties of fulfilling this in Morocco, and my agenda changed.

My understanding of the depth of the problem began when I realised Morocco had *not* adopted the successful drug addiction and alcohol recovery programmes, Narcotics Anonymous (NA) and Alcoholics Anonymous (AA). These along with their sister fellowships for families and friends, Al-Anon, Nar-Anon and Families Anonymous (FA) have already helped millions recover, including over 600,000 Muslims in the MENA Region.

But my real understanding of the depth of Morocco's drug problems began when I first read 'The National Observatory on Drugs and Addiction' (ONDA) report about Morocco's drug issues. It was written two years earlier by Prof. Jallal Toufiq, Prof. El Omari, and Dr. Maria Sabir, who worked at the Ar-azi psychiatric hospital in Salé - Rabat.

As an overview and to the uninitiated, it may seem the ONDA report was good because it was long and detailed, but to anyone who knows about recovery from drug addiction, it was not. The solutions it proposed were theoretical, not practical. The results I witnessed every day on Morocco's city streets were no better than when it was published in 2014, and nine years later they are still the same.

This fact I realised is not surprising as the ONDA report makes no mention of drug addiction or alcoholism as diseases. Nor does it refer to Narcotics Anonymous or Alcoholics Anonymous, the most successful methods of drug and alcohol treatment in the world for the past 85 years.

Cynics would say this is for two reasons: Morocco's psychiatrists and doctors would not want to admit they are wrong, and as the NA and AA 12-Step programmes are free, their success would deprive these medical professionals of patients who provide them with substantial incomes.

One of the worst effects of this negligence is the everyday sight of drug-addicted street children dressed in rags aged 7 to 15. The first time I saw some of Morocco's 10,000 drug-addicted street children was in Grand Socco, Tangier's main square. It was 3 p.m. and I was having tea with friends outside its famous Rif cinema. There were people everywhere. Then, as if out of the blue, eight children appeared. The oldest was no more than 11, but most were aged 8 or 9. Each sniffed solvent from a filthy plastic bag.

24

Whether it was the effect of the drugs or lack of interest by the authorities, they were oblivious to what went on around them. They knew from experience no one would do anything about their anti-social behaviour. Whereas if this was in New York's Times Square, London's Piccadilly Circus, or on the Champs Elysees in Paris, the authorities responsible would be hung out to dry for allowing such inhumane heartlessness.

In the two years I spent living in Morocco and visits spread over more than thirty years, I came to realise there were street children everywhere. When I questioned people about this, it became obvious nothing significant is done to help them. In my travels from Chefchaouen in the north, to Rabat, Casablanca, Kenitra, and Marrakech in the middle, and Agadir in the south, I witnessed these distressing images. This is not surprising as it is estimated there are 70,000 street children in Morocco; at least 10,000 of whom are already drug addicts!

To endeavour to understand this and try to put it right I had lunch with the most revered psychiatrist involved in drug addiction treatment in Morocco, Prof. Jallal Toufiq. As he was the main author of the ONDA report and the son of Morocco's Minister of Islamic Affairs, I took the view he may be able to persuade officials at the highest levels there are better ways to deal with the country's drug problems than the policies currently applied.

At the outset, I was encouraged as he indicated support for starting AA and NA at the hospital where he was a director. But I was equally discouraged when, at the end of our lunch, he proudly told me he had never taken an addictive mood-altering drug in his life.

I put this down to Islamic teachings and his father's position.

As I left our meeting I reflected on its pros and cons. Mostly my thoughts were positive, but I also wondered how a country practicing Islam could support its medical professionals by giving drug addicts and alcoholics strong, substitute, addictive drugs made by pharmaceutical firms.

On further reflection and at least as important, I recalled how the doctor who treated my alcoholism and drug addiction was six years clean and sober, plus he was a member of AA and NA. This gave him credibility; the exact opposite of what Prof. Toufiq would transmit when he talked to drug addicts or alcoholics. His lifelong abstinence would almost certainly be off-putting.

But worse was to come. The psychiatrist, Prof. Fatima El Omari who was chosen to start the Ar-azi hospital's AA meeting, seemed to have her own agenda. As soon as I found out what she was doing was wrong, I offered to help. As a result, she asked me to explain.

I did exactly that based on thousands of successful global AA start-ups in more than hundred and seventy-five countries. But Prof. El Omari ignored what I told her, and a few months later, I was told by another psychiatrist the meeting had closed.

Several times since I have tried to put this right by contacting Profs. El Omari and Toufiq, but both stopped replying. As their influence regarding addiction treatment in Morocco is substantial, this was and still is, a serious concern. It made me wonder, why don't they want to apply what is proven to be the best treatment for drug addicts and alcoholics? It was then I joined the cynics.

The result is that AA and NA solutions to alcoholism and drug addiction which work in every country where they are applied have not been given the opportunity in Morocco. Additionally, AA and NA's reputations as treatment solutions may have suffered as a result of the Ar-azi hospital failure, making it more difficult than it already is to get them established there in the future.

My negative attitude had been slightly aroused a few weeks earlier. Prof. Mehdi Paes, former head of Ar-azi Hospital, invited me to attend Morocco's annual psychiatrists and psychotherapists convention in Rabat. As a social event, this was fine, but nothing I heard that day would remedy the countries' underlying drug problems. What I did hear would at best be temporary fixes.

Not long after, my view was capped when I met two Moroccan former alcoholic women from the UK who were visiting their families in Casablanca. Thanks to working the AA programmes in London, each of these women was over fifteen years in recovery.

So, I asked them to help.

To my surprise they refused. When I asked why they explained they did not want their families to know of their former alcohol problem. The stigma and shame - *hshouma* - of being an alcoholic or drug addict in Morocco, especially a woman, was the reason. They did not know one another, while the experience each shared with me, I soon found out was common to *all* Moroccans; and if you are gay or lesbian, it is worse.

A key aspect of all 12-Step recovery programmes is to help others with the same problem. As this was the first time, I had encountered this attitude in thirty-five years in any of the countries I had been to, it meant I needed to add **hshouma** to the difficulties of establishing NA and AA in Morocco.

In each of the thirty-four countries I had visited where I met alcoholics and drug addicts, they too suffered stigmatisation. But in Morocco, it often seemed beyond redemption. Once I realised this, I dedicated my efforts to understanding the reasons, otherwise, there would be no likelihood of establishing NA and AA there.

Reflecting on all my experience I found was the best place to start.

Drug addiction and alcoholism are diseases, and until Morocco's medical professionals make this clear to the authorities and public, and treat them as such, the stigma that shackles its addicts and alcoholics to the drug substitution regime they have adopted will persist. And if this continues, drug addicts and alcoholics who live there will never receive the best treatment.

Because of their global diaspora over five million Moroccans live abroad. This means that today many are *drug addicts and alcoholics living outside Morocco who are in recovery*. That is because countries, where they live, such as France, Spain, the UK, USA, Netherlands, Italy, Canada, and Belgium, provide the NA and AA programmes that deal with the root causes of their disease. From then on, they practice living in the solution also provided by NA and AA, which means they can stay drug and alcohol-free for as long as they live.

If this happened in Morocco, the same should apply. Then, many of that country's drug-addicted men and women would recover, and the principles of 12-step recovery programmes be passed on to its drug-addicted street children.

Another benefit would be that this would stop much crime. A lot of inmates in Morocco's prisons start as street children created by Morocco's drug policies, hypocritical drug laws, and ineffective addiction treatment. This means such juveniles never get the opportunity to stop their criminal or anti-social behaviour.

However, there may be an answer.

Moroccans who live abroad contribute around €10 billion annually to their families and society back in Morocco. If these benefactors were made aware of the damage caused by Morocco's wayward drug policies, they might not be so generous. With this huge financial resource drying up and backlash of adverse publicity, it could put pressure on Morocco's authorities to change its policies to those that work.

There are other reasons too for Morocco's deep-rooted *hshouma*. One of these is based on the reasons Moroccans first left the country: poverty, and no likelihood of employment.

In April 2023 the World Bank released its Poverty and Equity Brief, which forecast that poverty and vulnerability are set to increase from its already very low levels in Morocco, notably in rural areas.

Another reason for the shame some people have of being Moroccan is caused by King Mohamed VIth's lifestyle and behaviour. The obliviousness this demonstrates seems to show a lack of concern for his country's poorest citizens and proletariat. It is reflected in his image of the outside world. In France, home to nearly 1.5 million Moroccans, where he spends much time, he is known as the 'king of the poor'.

Even though the king benefits from huge state financial support for his palaces and homes in Morocco, he spends much of his time at a palace he owns near Paris, he also goes to France for medical treatment and to seemingly indulge in a hedonistic lifestyle. At the same time, he is also renowned for his collections of cars, watches, and other non-essential material assets.

These aspects of his character have not only led to a lack of respect but many challenge the claim he is a direct descendent of Muhammad the Prophet, founder of Islam. Whereas, if he spread his estimated €1 billion annual earnings to Moroccans who desperately need help, it would improve his reputation and the country's image.

Normally a person is proud to say where they come from, but for Moroccans, this does not always seem to be the case. Those who live, travel, or study abroad, follow social media or Western news, are aware of what they think are better policies and opportunities elsewhere. These include higher standards of living, freedom of speech, equal rights for women, the legality of being lesbian or homosexual, and superior medical treatment.

Wherever they are Moroccans know their homeland is an autocracy where such freedoms and conditions do not exist, while there are vast chasms between the rich and poor. They also know beggars and street children exist in every village, town, and city, and that Moroccan drug laws and policies have fuelled some Moroccans to be responsible for some of the worst crimes in Europe this century.

Putting it all together it is possible to understand why it is difficult for some Moroccans not to have pride in their country.

This belief sadly can only add to some peoples' *hshouma.*

Chapter 2

Effects and causes of Morocco's Drug issues.

To understand them better, I made a list of the worst effects of Morocco's drug issues. It was longer than I expected, and it surprised me because all except the first were unique.

a. The treatment given to alcoholics and drug addicts in Morocco is inefficient, often making their long-term condition worse.

b. It's politicians and medical professionals need to ask the question, 'Why are there more *recovered* Moroccan former drug addicts in each of the Netherlands, France, Belgium, UK, USA and Spain, than in *the whole of* Morocco?

c. There are thousands of drug-addicted solvent-sniffing children aged 7 to 15 living on Morocco's streets. A fact unknown in most of the rest of the world.

d. By Morocco not dealing with its extremes of poverty, it has created the need for its infamous drug, *karkoubi*. Known as 'the drug of mass destruction' and 'drug of the poor', because using it has horrendous social and criminal consequences and it is very cheap.

e. Moroccan links to drugs and radicalisation have influenced the worst terrorist attacks in France, Spain, United Kingdom, Belgium and Morocco this century, while 1,659 of its citizens joined ISIS. Why?

f. Moroccan, Mounir al-Motassadek was the only person convicted and imprisoned because of his involvement in the 9/11 World Trade Centre and Pentagon attacks in 2001 that killed 3000 people.

g. Morocco is a hub for drug trafficking Afghanistan's heroin, South American cocaine, and its home-grown cannabis to Europe.

h. The Netherlands' powerful Moroccan mafia – the Mocro-Maffia - is drug financed and responsible for much-organised crime in Europe.

Putting the effects together, I understood the extent of the problems caused by Morocco's drug policies. I was then able to conclude it was what its politicians and medical professionals had done in the past, and still do, in relation to drug policies and addiction treatment that were the main causes. So, unless this changes, more of the same must be expected.

But knowing the effects of Morocco's links to drugs did not answer the question. 'Why are many Moroccans radicalised into acts of terrorism and go into organised crime?'

To address this conundrum, I considered the known reasons and causes.

Reasons for Radicalisation

A widespread view is that economic factors, particularly poverty and inequality, are driving causes of radicalisation, while political manipulation is considered a contributing factor.

Radicalisation is when someone starts to believe or support extreme views, and in some cases, then participates in terrorist groups or acts. It can be motivated by a range of factors, including ideologies, religious beliefs, political beliefs, and prejudices against specific groups of people. Those radicalised may be influenced in various ways, and over different time frames from as little as a few days or weeks, to several years.

Anyone can be radicalised, but factors such as being easily influenced and impressionable make children and young people particularly vulnerable. Those at risk may also have low self-esteem or be victims of bullying or discrimination. In many cases, they feel,

a.   isolated and lonely or want to belong.
b.   unhappy about themselves and what others think of them.
c.   embarrassed or judged about their culture, gender, religion or race.
d.   stressed or depressed.
e.   fed up with being bullied or treated badly at home, by other people or society.
f.   angry at other people or the government.
g.   confused about what they are doing.
h.   pressured to stand up for other people who are being oppressed.
i.   hatred as many live in extreme poverty.

Causes of Morocco's Drug Problems

1.   Morocco applies the rest of the world's drug laws, but they have distorted them to suit dubious agendas.

2.   Morocco is the world's largest producer of cannabis resin (source UN), yet it is illegal there!

3.   Many Moroccans are illiterate and extremely poor, so they use cheap, drugs to pacify themselves. This includes hundreds of thousands of uneducated street

children sniffing solvents, cannabis and the notorious drug, *karkoubi*. An official report in 2022 found social disparities between rich and poor regarding education were deepening. In 2023 the soaring rise in the cost of living in Morocco has caused widespread demonstrations. Over 130,000 drop out of school every year.

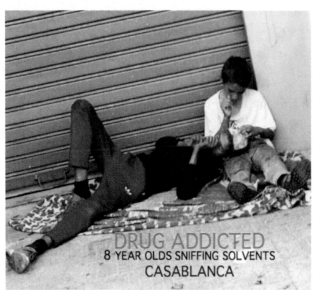

Photo at traffic lights 300 meters from Casablanca's 20th August 1953 hospital addiction unit.

Drug addicted children who later turn to *karkoubi* are easily radicalised.

4   Morocco has a huge black market. This stretches from dealing in prescription drugs like methadone, Subutex, Suboxone, Rivotril, tranquilisers, sleeping pills and anti-depressants to illicit drugs.

5   A seemingly politically motivated 'let's pacify them' regime is aimed at preventing crime and anti-social behaviour. A policy that pays no heed to the effect it has on the health of addicts, their families or society in the long term.

6   Morocco has extremes of rich and poor. From billionaires like its King and Prime Minister, wealthy government officials, medical professionals and drug lords, to some of the poorest families on earth. Such divides fester resentment, social unrest, and attraction to drugs.

7   As well as rich drug lords, hundreds of thousands of Moroccans depend on cannabis to support their families. The problem now is that destroying its cannabis industry would cause more poverty, and social unrest.

8   Morocco has over 1,000,000 drug addicts and alcoholics *not in recovery.* Each person is tagged a lawbreaker or criminal. Many commit the worst type of crimes, destroy their families, fill prisons, and hospitals, and cause accidents.

9   Morocco is ranked third in the world for road accident deaths behind America and China. When population sizes are compared, this statistic is unbelievable, unless you have lived there! (Morocco World News.)

10   If Morocco's drug addicts and alcoholics practice the NA and AA 12-Step recovery programmes, many of its 1,000,000+ drug and alcohol abusers would no longer commit crimes or anti-social behaviour. Adopting them, therefore, is essential: if only 500,000 recover – as is the case in Iran – such acts would be decimated, and huge savings made.

11   Morocco's policy of pacifying addicts puts them on prescription drugs which *prevent* recovery. Abstinence-based programmes, such as NA and AA, show success in helping millions recover including 600,000 in other Muslim countries. This should mean they will work in Morocco.

12   Morocco's government's policy may partly be due to the fear of reprisals from drug lords if it supports free abstinence programmes. Death threats to its medical profession have been reported.

13   As Morocco's doctors and psychiatrists do not treat addiction as a *disease,* this has led to a lack of understanding by families, society, and pharmacists. That causes another problem because admitting it after so long will be hard to explain. But it must be done.

14   Pharmaceutical companies providing drugs in Morocco incentivise doctors not to change prescribing habits by giving them expenses paid visits to exotic places.

15   Morocco's health services are internationally regarded as poor, while its king goes to France to be treated when he is sick!

16   Morocco's kings have autocratically presided over the country's policies. Until 2017 it had lèse–majesté laws. This meant it was a criminal offence to speak badly of a king's policy or him. Such acts resulted in a prison sentence of up to 5 years. The legacy is that Moroccans are still reluctant to speak negatively of his behaviour for fear of reprisals.

17   Morocco's interpretations of the Qur'an seem biased as mood-altering addictive drugs – narcotics - are prescribed by its medical profession and alcohol is sold everywhere with taxes applied that support the government.

18   The *root cause* of addiction *must* be treated for an addict or alcoholic to recover. Moroccans are not told this or offered the treatment to do it.

19   Morocco's policies and attitudes to drugs are the cause of the deep stigma and disgrace - *hshouma* – of being a drug addict or alcoholic. This makes the admission needed by the addict or alcoholic to recover difficult.

20   There are known medicinal benefits to cannabis. So, would a God of peace and love be unlikely to bless a country with the perfect geology and climate to grow it if God did not want it used for healing purposes? (It was not until 2021 Morocco acknowledged this and began to do something about it, and that it seemed was more for financial reasons!)

21   It is believed the Islamophobic behaviour of the American, British, French, and Spanish incentivised the Moroccans who committed the terrorist attacks in Madrid, Paris, London, Barcelona, and Brussels.

22   1,659 Moroccans joined the terrorist group ISIS. A disproportionally large number considering the size of Morocco's population.

****

Moroccan Links to Terrorist Attacks.

To understand the reasons behind Morocco's links to this century's terrorist attacks, I needed to go back to the 20th of March 2003, the day the American-led coalition invaded Iraq.

UN weapons inspectors worked in Iraq from November 27, 2002, until March 18, 2003. During that time, they conducted over 900 inspections at more than 500 sites. The inspectors did not find that Iraq possessed chemical or biological weapons or that it had a nuclear weapons program. Even so, the United States ignored the inspectors' results, abandoned the inspection process, and initiated the invasion of Iraq on March 19.

Had the world's people known the full extent of the political shenanigans behind this invasion, and the horror of the terrorist attacks it would later influence, the number of people who demonstrated against it would not have been the millions that did, it would have been hundreds of millions.

As early as May 16th of the same year, the invasion caused suicide bombings with only brief breaks in between that have taken place since.

They began in Casablanca, while other deadly attacks have taken place in Madrid, Paris, Marrakesh, London, Brussels, and Barcelona.

This prompts the question, where will be next, and how many more people must die before what needs to be done to stop them is put in place?

Although the attack that opened my eyes to the situation was in 2003, it was not until hundreds more had died, and thousands were injured in the other attacks, I knew the reasons and what needed to be done to stop them.

Chapter 3

Total Abstinence vs Harm Reduction

The pharmaceutical industry is, *"getting away with murder...... Pharma has a lot of lobbies, a lot of lobbyists and a lot of power......We're the largest buyer of drugs (in the world)."* So said Donald Trump in his first speech as President-elect of the USA.

Although for many people it would be hard to support anything he stood for, this statement encapsulates much truth as it inadvertently acknowledges some less-known facts.

While Mr Trump was referring to prices and consumption of the pharmaceutical industry's legal drugs, what he said also gives way to people asking if a similar statement could be made about the deaths caused by their prescription drug substitutes. As well as misinformation about pain killers, anti-depressants, and benzodiazepines passed on to doctors by medical representatives working for such firms?

To help minimise the spread of HIV in the 1980s from the use of dirty needles and syringes, the practice of 'harm reduction' was introduced. It is described as a strategy that aims to reduce the harms associated with certain behaviours by individuals and some groups of people. When applied to illegal drugs, prescription drug abuse, and alcohol, it accepts that continuing levels in society are inevitable; so, it defines its objective as only reducing adverse consequences.

Because the marketing term 'harm reduction' sounds good, it has been applied by the pharmaceutical industry, politicians, and police to convince people this was the best way to prevent drug abusers from committing anti-social behaviour. As a result, many doctors began to 'pacify' drug abusers of all types with substitute mood-altering addictive drugs made by Big-Pharma and others in that industry.

This may seem like a good thing, but to former drug addicts and alcoholics who are abstinent from all drugs, it is not. They live by the principle of, 'one drug is too many, a thousand is never enough'.

It is clear from this example that there is a big difference between the drug substitution approach - harm reduction and total abstinence. As the consequences for families and society are also huge, it is essential that only the best treatment is applied.

As the doctrine of drug substitution has become widely used in the past thirty-five years, it is important to examine why, when in nearly 180 countries there was already a proven free treatment of total abstinence that worked which had existed for over eighty years.

One way to do this is to compare the results of drug policies in countries that have the worst drug problems, to those that have the best. As there are extreme examples of these, this is relatively easy.

From pacify to crucify, has been an effect of Morocco's past drug addiction treatment policies, which are almost exclusively harm reduction and drug substitution. The result is Morocco continues to have serious drug problems at home, while its countrymen who committed terrorist attacks in Madrid, Barcelona, Paris, London, and Brussels, invariably had links to drugs, as do the Moroccans involved in organised crime in the Netherlands. Known as the 'Mocro-Maffia', it is financed by Moroccan cannabis and drug trafficking.

The crucify factor would have been unintentional. However, when medical reps told Morocco's doctors and psychiatrists about the use of harm reduction in other countries, they would not have mentioned its killer knock-on effect on drug addicts and alcoholics. To them it was a policy being introduced all over the world for which they were not responsible; though it did directly and financially benefit them and the pharmaceutical firms they worked for hugely financially.

At the same time, Portugal's results regarding drug-associated problems went from bad to good. This was because its government decriminalised drugs and gave financial support to addiction treatment facilities, while the successful 12-Step recovery programmes of Alcoholics Anonymous (AA) and Narcotics Anonymous (NA) spread throughout the country.

These results alone should mean policymakers and doctors consider what they do, removing policies that do not work with ones that do. But, for the people who make pharmaceutical drugs, maintaining these policies and laws is important. Therefore, unless they are forced to, self-interest means they will not make changes to regimes they instigated, even when at times they are causing a shocking waste of life.

As in Morocco's case, these include its king, politicians, police, and medical professionals, it would be difficult to challenge or denounce them. Yet that is what must be done.

Although the country's drug laws and policies are much to blame, so too are the mood-altering addictive drugs its doctors prescribe to substitute other drugs, or numb pain. This is because, although they are addictive and dangerous, they are not called 'narcotic', which is also true of alcohol. These substitute 'narcotics' include tranquillisers such as Valium prescribed to treat anxiety and the opiates, methadone, Subutex and Suboxone used to treat heroin addiction and others such as fentanyl and Oxycontin, to combat acute pain. *Plus ça change, plus c'est la même chose*!

For more than a hundred years, practices adopted by politicians, pharmaceutical firms, police, and the media have duped both doctors and the public. First prohibition, then the 'war on drugs', and now drug substitution and harm reduction have all been adopted to rectify drug problems. Retrospectively we know such regimes do not work. As with any disease, only treatments that deal with root causes work.

There is a treatment for drug addiction that when applied does precisely that; it starts by recognising that all forms of addiction are diseases. By educating the public and medical profession with this fact, with sufficient pressure, politicians and the police would find it hard not to fall in line.

As it was the same authorities, plus the pharmaceutical industry that introduced harm reduction using drug substitution to do the same, it was assumed this must be good. But as people now know the pharmaceutical industry cannot be trusted; this century's multi-billion-dollar lawsuits against them prove their tactics and claims need careful examination. All too often we see making money was their aim, regardless of the cost to human life and society.

An example of this is the pharmaceutical group GlaxoSmithKline (GSK). In 2012, GSK was fined US$ 3 billion after admitting to bribing doctors and encouraging the prescription of unsuitable antidepressants to two million children. The company encouraged sales representatives in the US to mis-sell three drugs to doctors, and lavished hospitality and favours on those who agreed to write extra prescriptions - including expenses paid trips to Bermuda, Jamaica and California. In court the company admitted corporate misconduct over the antidepressants Seroxat (Paxil), and Wellbutrin and the asthma drug, Advair.

But still, 'harm reduction' sounds good and representatives of the pharmaceutical industry were still able to persuade doctors and psychiatrists to trust it. They omitted to tell them there are **free** alternatives that have worked to help millions of drug addicts and alcoholics recover, and to remain permanently abstinent in most countries in the world. They and the firms they work for, prefer to sell their expensive and addictive substitute drugs that need replenishing repeatedly, which makes them huge profits.

The results of harm reduction seem to indicate it has not significantly improved anything, and for many drug addicts it has made their problems worse. Crime and anti-social behaviour committed by active drug and alcohol abusers continues. This means the consequences for *victims* stays the same. This is reflected in the continuing societal and familial problems, while the millions of sufferers of the diseases of drug addiction or alcoholism have not been given the best opportunity to recover.

Globally, the millions of recovered drug addicts and alcoholics who are *abstinent of all drugs,* are proof of these changes of behaviour. While anyone who questions it, needs only consider the dishonesty behind America's hundreds of thousands of opiate overdose deaths. These being a direct result of pharmaceutical representatives' mis-selling drugs and doctors' mis-prescribing them.

Arthur Sackler was co-founder of Purdue pharmaceuticals. I knew him personally as he married a good friend in London. To sell its Oxycontin opiate (narcotic), Purdue marketed it in much the same way it marketed Valium a few years earlier. But OxyContin was always a controversial drug; its sole active ingredient oxycodone is a chemical cousin of heroin which is up to twice as powerful as morphine.

When it was discovered that aggressive mis-selling of Oxycontin was responsible for hundreds of thousands of overdose deaths in America, lawsuits were established on behalf of *victim's* families. As the result, Purdue closed down, while the Sackler family made US$ billion's settlements.

Although none of the Sackler's faced criminal charges and denied any wrongdoing, their alleged role in pushing opioid (narcotic drugs) sales resulted in a public backlash. The family previously portrayed as art loving philanthropists, now had the Sackler name removed from museums, universities, and art institutions around the world. Then, in October 2021, the TV series 'Dopesick' made clear how the Purdue *victims* had suffered. All the while the Sackler family and its directors were only interested in making fortunes. This left many people thinking the family and its directors should have been dealt with more severely by the courts.

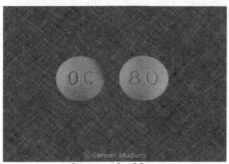
Oxycontin 80 mg

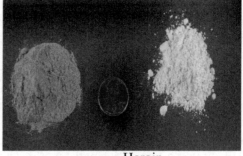
Heroin

In the 1960s Purdue's marketing strategy transformed a diazepam, better known as Valium, into a blockbuster. From being just another drug produced by his client, Hoffman-La Roche, Arthur helped turn it into one of the USA's top-selling 'wonder' drugs. When I discovered this occurred between 1968 and 1982, it rang a huge bell.

On the 1st of August 1985, I was lying on a bed in a coma in Charter Clinic on Primrose Hill in London. This was the result of taking a daily dose of Hoffman-La Roche's Valium, first prescribed to me by a doctor in Birmingham years earlier. I had been twenty-one years old at that time and was working for Cadbury's chocolate manufacturers.

To begin with, I took 2 mg twice a day to treat pain in my abdomen. I later discovered it was caused by eating too much chocolate, with nothing at all to do with anxiety! By the age of thirty-two, I was a chronic alcoholic and my daily intake of Valium had risen to over 40 mg a day. I was now a prescription drug 'junkie' and an alcoholic.

To treat this, the next eight years involved another doctor and two psychiatrists switching me from Valium to the much stronger and more dangerous benzodiazapine, Ativan. As my dependence grew, so did my tolerance. By the age of forty I was drinking between 3 and 5 bottles of wine, spirits and beer a day:

taking a minimum 150 mgs of tranquillisers, and 3 to 5 Mogadon sleeping pills at night.

In other words, lethal legal drugs made by the largest companies in the world, in the brewing and pharmaceutical industries, helped turn a law-abiding young man into an alcoholic and prescription drug addict.

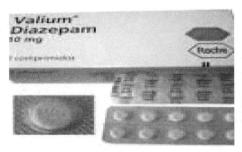
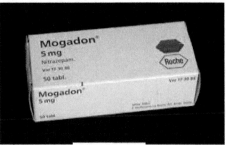

Valium by Roche

Mogadon by Roche

Although I am not suggesting there has been any wrongdoing by Roche, it is imperative that their sales and marketing personnel take precautions to prevent this or any misunderstandings by anyone prescribing or using them. They have that responsibility as their mood-altering addictive drugs are market leaders and misuse can be dangerous.

However, there was another bell regarding Roche's drugs that when I first heard it rang even louder.

After I had lived in Morocco for a few months, I was told about the drug cocktail, *Karkoubi*, probably more dangerous than any other in the world. It is exclusive to Morocco and known as *'the drug of mass destruction'* and *'drug of the poor'*. What registered with me was not just its effect when taken with alcohol that causes users to commit the most heinous crimes, it was its ingredients: solvent, cannabis, and benzodiazepine. The latter was Rivotril made by Roche.

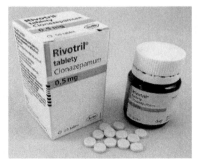

Rivotril

Karkoubi containing Rivotril

40

A few weeks later I was in Madrid doing research for a book about Morocco's links to terrorism and organised crime. A pharmacist told me that recently every pharmacy in Spain was sent an official letter from their governing body concerning prescription drug forgeries; invariably they were for Rivotril. These would then be smuggled to Morocco to make *Karkoubi*. This was in 2018.

Estimado compañero: La inspección sanitaria de la Consejería de Sanidad de la Comunidad de Madrid nos ha informado de que existen varios talonarios falsos circulando y que dan error al escanearlos a través de SISCATA.

En general son prescripciones del medicamento RIVOTRIL 2 mg y los números de dichos talonarios son:

MD4 3265023

MD4 3265024

MD4 3265025

En el caso de que recibas una receta que te dé error en su escaneo en SISCATA y corresponda a uno de estos talonarios, te recomendamos que no realices la dispensación. Recibe un cordial saludo,

Óscar López Moreno
Vocal de Titulares de Oficina de Farmacia
vocalia.farmacia@cofm.es
Santa Engracia, 31 6ª planta
28010 Madrid Tel. 91 406 83 83

When I became a business development advisor to the pharmaceutical industry in the 1990s, I was shocked to discover that mis-selling was relatively common; profits came first. It was only later I found out it was profit that had incentivised nefarious marketing tactics to promote Purdue's Oxycontin.

As Purdue was the leading marketer of Valium, I now wondered if such tactics had been used to market that too. After all, the timing was right, and I was prescribed it for pain in my abdomen!

From that moment on I no longer trusted the pharmaceutical industry.

****

There are effective ways to compare the results of total abstinence programmes with harm reduction by drug substitution. One is to look at the short, medium and long-term effects with regard to recovery from alcoholism and drug addiction.

As there are several million recovered drug addicts and alcoholics who applied the 12-Step recovery programmes of NA and AA spread across the world, this is a good place to start.

From the moment a drug addict or alcoholic starts to apply an NA or AA programme, several things happen. The identification they get talking to clean and sober former addicts or alcoholics means they no longer feel alone. Then they realise that at no financial cost, they have become part of a global fellowship of people just like them, some of whom are now blessing them with a love and understanding they have not encountered before.

What is more, these are new friends who will be there whenever they need them until they are able to look after themselves. And wherever they travel at home or abroad, there will be others just like them to support and guide them. There are also other benefits.

From this time on it is unlikely any of these former miscreants will ever be a practicing criminal again, or a risk to society or their families; working through each 12-Step programme virtually guarantees this. Plus, they will not cause alcohol or drug induced traffic accidents or require visits to doctors or pharmacists to deal with addiction or need expensive drug substitutes; and if they need a hospital bed, it will be for a non-drug related reason.

Invariably they become workers, and as their abilities range from being doctors, lawyers, teachers, nurses, police officers, social workers, manual labourers, politicians, authors and artists, to sport, television, movie. music and pop superstars, and every job or profession in between, the benefits to humanity are enormous.

12-Step programmes are based on spiritual, but not religious, principles. They are open to anyone regardless of religion, lack of religion, colour, race or sexual identity. People who apply them learn new practices for living. Such as prayer, meditation and serving others without financial reward. Invariably this leads to an awakening of an individual's spirit and an incredible camaraderie.

Finally, if instead recovering addicts are put on drug substitutes, they will be deprived of the many priceless benefits a life of total abstinence provides; they will always see the world through a prism distorted by drugs.

If harm reduction is applied, they will not deal with the underlying issues that cause their addiction problem. This means they may remain dishonest, not make amends for previous wrongdoings, not return to work, and worst of all, when faced with difficulties they may relapse on their previous drug or drugs. Many then die, end up in hospital or in an institution. The support they get will be from drugs and the people who administer them at considerable cost, potentially to their health, and financially to the state.

For anyone who doubts this, there are examples to consider if it is true. Iran and Morocco are one comparison, probably better than any, that shows how hundreds of thousands of addicts' lives have been saved versus virtually none.

Iran has a population of approximately 88,000,000 people. The main illicit drug there is opium, which comes from nearby Afghanistan. It is estimated to have the highest per capita number of opioid addicts in the world at a rate of 2.8% of Iranians over age 15. Its government estimates the number of such addicts is two million.

In 1993 two Americans started the free, abstinence-only, programme, NA there. Today there are more than 500,000 former Iranian drug addicts in recovery spread across the country. On a per-head basis, this makes Iran the most successful country in the world for recovered drug addicts.

Morocco on the other hand has 1,200,000 practicing drug addicts and alcoholics, thousands of whom are solvent-sniffing children who go on to be hard drug users and criminals. Its medical professionals have exclusively used harm reduction to treat them. The result is, in the whole country, there are less than a dozen Moroccan addicts who are abstinent of all drugs.

It is little wonder, therefore, that Morocco's drug problems rank it with the worst in the world, *though probably it has the worst!*

What is extraordinary is that Morocco has not stopped the practices that cause its problems. Psychiatrists, many of whom know better, have not supported the establishment of NA and AA, or helped to remove the social stigma of being a drug addict, while its politicians have not done what they should to get rid of poverty. If Morocco took these steps, it would mean more foreign businesses would want to establish themselves there and more tourists would visit.

But it is most likely there will be more of the same until there is another Moroccan-influenced terrorist attack. When that happens, Morocco's king and its government's negligence will be highlighted. However, the wrongdoings of the pharmaceutical industry and politicians in many countries would be as well.

If such action is withheld, those responsible will have failed in their duty, because the people they represent will suffer. You cannot disconnect its effects from society. The apathetic omission of the **villains** should call forth the condemnation of all far-sighted citizens and those **victims** who follow. One more such tragedy will be too many, but more will be likely.

The future results of such positive action could propagate other countries to do the same. Then, who knows, maybe King Mohamed VIth and Morocco's leading psychiatrist, Jallal Toufiq, may be nominated for the Nobel Peace Prize.

But sadly, there is a long way to go for both them and the country before that happens.

****

Footnote.

After reading this chapter, ask yourself two questions, while remembering that the man who wrote it, along with millions of other alcoholics and drug addicts, would have been dead years ago if the doctors who treated their disease had not guided them to apply the best possible treatment.

1. If you had a son or daughter, sister or brother, father or mother, wife or husband who is a chronic alcoholic or drug addict, would you not want them to have the best treatment to conquer their condition?

2. To treat drug addiction or alcoholism, which has the best results, total abstinence, or harm reduction?

    Answering honestly seems to indicate these questions are no-brainers. So, the next questions need to be,

3. Why are there so many instances when doctors do not apply the *best* treatment for drug addicts and alcoholics?

4. Why are there countries that do not support the *best* treatment?

5. Who are the *villains*? We know the *victims*.

Chapter 4

Madrid Bombings 2004

Eulogio Paz Fernandez is President of the Victims of Terrorism Association and father of Daniel, aged 20. Daniel was among 190 others killed in the Madrid bomb attacks on 11 March 2004. Senor Fernandez directly blames Spain's Prime Minister, José María Aznar for their deaths.

He and millions of others are convinced, that in addition to the terrorists, the political leaders at the time in the USA, United Kingdom, and Spain were responsible. In a speech to victims' families, he said that if Aznar had not involved Spain in the Iraq war, his son would be alive today. Aznar had led Spain into a war that was overwhelmingly disapproved of by the people of Spain, plus the millions who demonstrated against it in America and the UK.

Protagonists Tony Blair, George Bush, and Jose Maria Aznar.

While the denial of this by each of them knew no bounds, people still believed they all had personal agendas. To many Spaniards, Aznar's agenda seemed to have been more important than any backlash against Spain.

In April 1995, he was wounded in a car bombing that was attributed to the Basque separatist group ETA. So, when it came to attributing blame for the Madrid bomb attacks, despite **all** the evidence pointing against it, he put his and his colleagues' efforts into blaming ETA. This persisted even though after just a few days it was obvious it was not ETA, but an Arab-influenced attack. This resulted in his political party being removed in an election three days later and his reputation tarnished for life with millions of Spanish people and on the global stage.

At Atocha station, the destination of the four trains that were attacked, an 11m (36 ft) high commemorative memorial cylinder stands above it. This was the main location where terrorists killed 193 people and injured around 2000 on 11th March 2004.

Texts composed of expressions of grief in many languages sent in the days after the attack from all over the world are printed on a clear colourless membrane that is inflated by air pressure. The structure is composed of glass blocks and sits on a platform above. The light in the blue room below comes from this source alone. At night it is illuminated by lamps within its base and can be seen throughout the station's surroundings. Visiting it is a moving experience.

Inside the Atocha Station Memorial

To commemorate the 193 victims, olive and cypress trees were planted for each person killed in Madrid's Bueno Retiro Park, known as The Forest of Remembrance. Although this feature and the plaque that was added are a place of beauty and love, for visitors who know the truth behind the attacks, many leave with feelings of bitterness as well as sadness.

Forest of Remembrance, Bueno Retiro Park, Madrid

Investigators believe that each blast was caused by improvised explosive devices packed in backpacks that were taken aboard the trains. The terrorists targeted Atocha Station and the nearby area, where seven of the bombs were detonated. The other bombs were detonated aboard trains near the El Poso del Tio Raimundo and Santa Eugenia stations, most likely because of delays in the trains' journeys on their way to Atocha Station. Three other bombs did not detonate and were later found intact.

Many in Spain and around the world saw the attacks as retaliation for Spain's participation in the Iraq war, where about 1,400 Spanish soldiers were stationed at the time. The attacks took place just days before a major Spanish election, in which anti-war Socialists rose to power. The new government, led by Prime Minister Jose Luis Rodriguez Zapatero, removed Spanish troops from Iraq, with the last leaving the country in May 2004.

A second bombing of a track of the high-speed AVE train was attempted on April 2nd but was unsuccessful. The next day, Spanish police linked the occupants of an apartment in Leganes, south of Madrid, to the attack. In the ensuing raid, seven suspects killed themselves and one Spanish special forces agent by setting off bombs in the apartment to avoid capture. One other bomber is believed to have been killed in the train bombings and 29 were arrested. After a five-month-long trial in 2007, 21 people were convicted, while five of them, including Rabei Osman, the alleged ringleader, were later acquitted.

For both the 11th March and April 2nd attacks, the main perpetrators were Moroccans.

As well as the commemorative monuments at Atocha station and in Bueno Retira Park, there are plaques at other sites where bombs exploded. In total, there were ten bombs on four trains in three Madrid-area train stations during the busy morning rush hour. They were later found to have been detonated by mobile phones. The most devastating terrorist attack in Europe since Lockerbie in 1988 when 270 people died.

Co-ordinated bomb attack memorial plaques Madrid 2004

Chapter 5

London Terrorist Attacks

On 7th July 2005 bomb blasts went off in three tunnels near the **Aldgate, Edgware Road, and Russell Square** underground stations in **London** within seconds of each other. In those deadly moments around 8:50 am, 39 people were killed. These were followed by another explosion an hour later which ripped a double-decker bus in two in **Tavistock Square**; that killed a further 13. In total, the four suicide bombers responsible murdered 52 people and injured over 700.

Double Decker Bus attack Tavistock Square

Hyde Park Memorial with names engraved for each victim.

Commemorative Plaque for victims outside the British Medical Association.

On 22 March 2017, a terrorist attack took place outside the **Palace of Westminster** in **London**, home of the British Parliament. A 52-year-old serial criminal known to take **steroids and cocaine,** drove a car into pedestrians on the south side of Westminster Bridge, injuring more than fifty people, four fatally. He then crashed the car and ran into New Palace Yard. He was shot by an armed police officer and died at the scene.

On 22nd May 2017, a terrorist of Libyan origin killed 22 people and injured 200 at an Ariana Grande concert in **Manchester.** He was a known **cannabis** user whose sister said he was influenced by the American-led attacks on Muslims.

The Glade of Light Memorial Manchester.

On 3rd June 2017, three terrorists deliberately drove a vehicle into pedestrians on **London Bridge**. They then crashed it and ran into the nearby Borough Market area and began stabbing people in and around restaurants and pubs. They were shot dead by police and found to be wearing fake explosive vests. Eight innocent people were killed and 48 were injured.

The ringleader of the terrorists was Khuram Butt, a British citizen born in Pakistan. His accomplices, Rachid Redouane and Youssef Zaghba were of **Moroccan** origin. At a pre-inquest hearing at the Old Bailey in February 2018 it was explained that all had **steroids** in their systems when they died. Toxicology reports said the levels were "above the acceptable physiological range" and had been taken "recently, prior to death."

Memorial plaque outside Southwark Cathedral to mark the fifth anniversary of the 3rd June 2017 London Bridge terrorist attack.

At 8-25 am on Friday 15th September 2017, a young Iraqi, Ahmed Hassan, was responsible for the detonation of a bomb on a Wimbledon to Earls Court, District Line train at **Parsons Green** station in **London.**

Acting alone, his homemade device, although it malfunctioned, injured 30 people, many suffering from terrible burns. The bomb was made of 400 gm of the explosive TAPT and kgs of nuts, bolts, and nails. Fortunately for passengers on this rush hour train, by not exploding properly, there were no fatalities. To save himself, Hassan got off the train at the previous Putney Bridge station having set a delay function on the bomb's timer.

Working at Parsons Green station that fateful morning was Dean Blanche, a station manager. Instantly he realised there had been some sort of catastrophe, his cool head had him issue a Code Red station shutdown. This meant that the fire service was there in 6 minutes, quickly followed by the police.

Equally important, Mr Blanche's spontaneous reaction meant the exit gates to the station automatically opened and stayed that way. Even though there were people panicking, and the platform and stairs were crowded, the station was evacuated in 12.5 minutes.

A terrorist with explosives enters the train

Contents nuts, bolts, and nails bomb

Chapter 6

Marrakesh Bombing 2011

Many countries have a place where the heart of their population seems to beat. For most visitors to Morocco, it is the massive souk next to Jemaa el-Fna square in Marrakesh.

Marrakesh is the most visited place by tourists to Morocco. Its souks selling leather goods, tagine pots, rugs, art, spices, lanterns, Moroccan slippers, and Arabic clothes are world famous. To get to the main souk, the most favoured way for tourists is through Jemaa el-Fna square, famous for its snake charmers. It is ringed by cafés and restaurants selling Moroccan mint tea and well-known dishes from its famous cuisine.

By mid-morning every day the square and main souk are alive with thousands of people. One of the most popular refreshment establishments in the square was the Argana restaurant, a tourist hotspot well-known for panoramic views. So, when at 11-50 am on April 29th? 2011, a lone Moroccan wearing Western clothes planted two bombs hidden inside a backpack, he did so un-noticed. He knew his actions would have the deadliest effect if successful, which they certainly were.

The devices he carried that fateful day killed 17 people, most of them foreign tourists, and injured 25. The dead victims were French, British, Portuguese, Swiss and Moroccan.

Since 20 February that year, there had already been three nationwide mass demonstrations for democracy and equality in Morocco, a country that has always been plagued by massive social injustice and a growing gap between the rich and the very poor.

Argana restaurant, Marrakesh, after a bomb killed 17 people and injured 25.

Police originally believed the al-Qaida terrorist network was behind the attack, but later concluded it was the work of a ringleader, Adel al-Othmani and six accomplices, most of whom were from the poor Moroccan Atlantic coast fishing port of Safi.

Like many things to do with law in Morocco, the sentencing of the terrorists that followed was controversial. A year after the attack, a Moroccan appeals court handed down much harsher sentences for the defendants than those when they were convicted in the previous court.

In addition to confirming the death sentence for the ringleader, al-Othmani, the appeals court changed the life sentence of his associate Hakim Dah also to capital punishment, too. While six other defendants convicted of being associated with the bombing had their prison sentences of two and four years increased to ten years. Only one defendant kept his original two-year sentence.

Legal experts in Morocco often criticise convictions based on flimsy evidence, especially in terrorism-related trials. In this case, it happened again. The defence attorneys were not allowed to call witnesses in the original trial, which was largely based on the confessions obtained by police. They claimed the case against their clients was based on statements coerced through torture and lacked hard evidence. Many of the defendants testifying said that they hardly knew al-Othmani.

An additional concern arose because France and Morocco at the time were close allies. Eight of the Marrakesh attack victims were French, and on the day the sentences were announced, the French Foreign Minister, Alain Juppe was visiting.

To the outside world and many Moroccans, especially those living in poverty, none of this looked good. In Morocco, it caused resentment towards the police and authorities; to the rest of the world, it confirmed suspicions that all is still not right in this kingdom where biased lèse-majesté obedience had always reigned.

Although in 2011 King Mohamed VIth had shifted some authority to the government from the monarchy, he still maintained dominance through a combination of substantial formal powers and informal lines of influence in the state and society. In practice, many civil liberties are constrained, making Morocco an authoritarian, not a democratic country.

Chapter 7

Paris Terrorist Attacks 2015

On 7 January 2015, four French Muslim terrorists, including two brothers, forced their way into the offices of the French satirical weekly newspaper Charlie Hebdo. In an attack almost identical to that in the film, 3 Days of the Condor, armed with rifles and other weapons, they murdered 12 people and injured 11 others. The gunmen identified themselves as belonging to 'the Islamic terrorist group', which took responsibility for the attack. During the next two days, related attacks followed in the Ile-de-France including a Jewish supermarket, where a terrorist murdered four Jews.

Plaque commemorating victims of Charlie Hebdo attack.

On Friday 13th November 2015, a series of coordinated terrorist attacks took place in central Paris and the city's northern suburb of Saint-Denis. 130 people were killed and 420 were injured, while 7 attackers also died. This made the attacks the deadliest in France since the Second World War, and the deadliest in the European Union since the Madrid train bombings in 2004.

Three suicide bombers struck outside the Stade de France during a football match between Germany and France. At around the same time, other attackers fired randomly in cafés and restaurants in the 13th Arrondissment, while another group carried out a mass shooting at an 'Eagles of Death Metal' concert attended by 1,500 people in the Bataclan theatre.

As this was the second such attack in Paris after Charlie Hebdo and the Jewish supermarket in January of the same year, France went on high terrorist alert. Its government then pledged €800 million to fund counterterrorism, which led to an increase in Islamophobic incidents. This was a worrying outcome as France is home to a large number of Muslims.

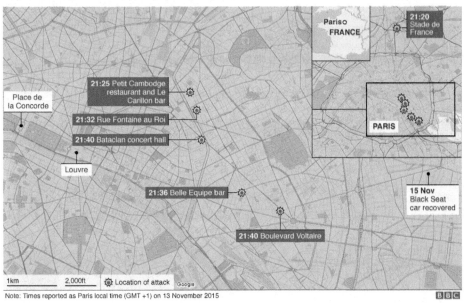

Sites of Paris attacks 13th November 2015

The attacks in and around Paris began around 9-30 pm, when a suicide bomber attempted to enter the Stade de France in Saint Denis. Inside, President Hollande was among the 80,000 people watching a football match between France and Germany. A security officer at one of the entrances detected the attacker's bomb belt, which he detonated killing a passer-by. It was later found to consist of the highly unstable explosive triacetone triperoxide, nails, and ball bearings; identical devices to those used by other attackers that night.

At approximately the same time, gunmen launched a series of attacks on popular nightspots in Paris's 10th and 11th arrondissements. The first to be targeted was Le Carillon, a bar on rue Alibert. After firing on patrons with AK-47 assault rifles, the gunmen crossed to Le Petit Cambodge on rue Bichat opposite, a Cambodian restaurant. These attacks lasted only a few minutes. They left 15 people dead, and many wounded. The gunmen left the scene in a black SEAT Leon.

Le Carillon and Le Petit Cambodge restaurants Rue Bichat and Rue Alibert

EN MÉMOIRE DES VICTIMES BLESSÉES
ET ASSASSINÉES DES ATTENTATS DU
13 NOVEMBRE 2015
AUX 13 VIES FAUCHÉES EN CES LIEUX

ALVA BERGLUND. CHLOÉ BOISSINOT. ASTA DIAKITE.
NOHEMI GONZALEZ. RAPHAEL HILZ. MOHAMED AMINE IBNOLMOBARAK.
CHARLOTTE ET EMILIE MEAUD. JUSTINE MOULIN.
MARION ET ANNA PETARD-LIEFFRIG. SÉBASTIEN PROISY.
STELLA SOANIRINA YASMINE VERRY.

Commémorative plaque for Le Carillon and Le Petit Cambodge attacks

The occupants of the black Leon then crossed into the 11th arrondissement and opened fire on businesses along the rue de la Fontaine au Roi. Five people were

58

killed and eight were wounded at the Italian restaurant La Casa Nostra, the Café Bonne Bière, and a laundromat. The gunmen then continued on to their next target.

La Belle Équipe is a popular restaurant on rue de Charonne. It was packed with diners, and the gunmen fired into the crowd, killing 19 people as well as critically wounding 9 others.

La Belle Equipe restaurant, Rue de Charonne, Paris

Commemorative wall of poppies in La Belle Equipe; one for each person who died, including the owner, Gregory Reinenberg's wife.

On Boulevard Voltaire, near La Belle Équipe, a suicide bomber detonated his belt outside Comptoir Voltaire (now Les Ogres) restaurant, injuring one person.

At the same time, at the other end of the Boulevard Voltaire, the deadliest attack of the evening happened at the Bataclan theatre and concert hall. The American rock band, Eagles of Death Metal, was playing to a capacity crowd of 1,500 when three attackers burst in and fired on the audience. Some of the concertgoers were able to escape through a side entrance, and dozens took refuge on the building's roof, while others hid or feigned death in an effort to avoid the attention of the gunmen.

Witnesses said the attackers shouted "Allāhu akbar" ("God is greatest") and anger at France's military intervention in Syria as the massacre continued. In total, The gunmen occupied the Bataclan for more than two hours, holding hostages and killing indiscriminately, before French security forces stormed the building at 12:20 AM. Two of the attackers detonated their suicide belts, and the third attacker's belt exploded spontaneously when it was hit with police bullets. Many at the concert goers were seriously wounded in the attack, and at least 89 people were killed.

Bataclan concert hall and plaque commemorating the victims.

As the attack at the Bataclan was taking place, fans at the Stade de France were becoming increasingly aware of the horrors outside the stadium. Sirens and police helicopters were audible, and a suicide bomber detonated his suicide-belt near the stadium. However, the stadiums' security management allowed the game to continue to prevent panic, so fans were prevented from leaving until it was believed it was safe to do so. This meant that although the match ended around 11:00 PM, it was not until after 11:30 PM fans were allowed to leave. In this time, as was done to thwart the German occupiers in the film, Casablanca, to raise morale, the crowd sang La Marseillaise, the French national anthem.

Chapter 8

Brussels Terrorist Attacks

The most devastating terrorist attacks in Belgium's history happened on 22nd March 2016. Three suicide bombers hit Brussels Zaventem airport and Maelbeek metro station, next to the European Commission. Using three homemade bombs packed with nails, 32 people were killed and nearly 350 were injured.

As well as the horrendous effects this had on thousands of lives, its nearness to the headquarters of the European Parliament in the Belgian capital meant it had ramifications across the whole of Europe. Where next was the obvious question?

On that occasion, two bombs were detonated in the departure hall of Brussels Airport around 8 am; a third bomb was later found unexploded in the same area. Shortly after 9 am, another bomb went off in the Brussels subway station of Maelbeek. The three suicide bombers who died at the time were later identified as Najim Laachraoui, Ibrahim el-Bakraoui at Brussels airport and Khalid el-Bakraoui at Maelbeek station. Each was a Moroccan Belgian and lived in Moleenbek, a poor district of Brussels.

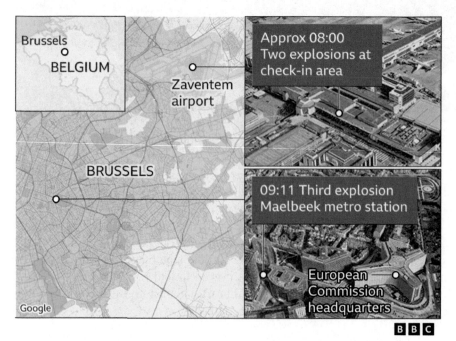

Locations of Brussels Terrorist Attacks 22nd March 2016

'I am Brussels' Commemorative Service and banner.

On 5th November 2022, nine alleged jihadists, including the cell's 32-year-old French - **Moroccan** ringleader, Saleh Abdeslam went on trial for a variety of charges. While one, who was thought to have been killed in Syria, was being tried in absentia.

In June 2022, six of the defendants, including Saleh Abdeslam were tried and found guilty of the Paris attacks in November 2015 that killed 130 people and injured 420.

Belgian-**Moroccan**, Mohamed Abrini, whose younger brother died after joining ISIS, twice drove the Abdeslam brothers from Brussels to Paris, and was seen at a petrol station on the way to Paris with Abdeslam the night of the attacks.

****

Food For Thought!

The European Policy Centre (EPC) report on terrorism shows how better policies could have prevented the radicalisation of many Moroccans into terrorism.

In March 2019, three years after the Brussels attack, the EPC published a report on terrorism. It explained how the European Union is taking steps to develop strategies that prevent radicalisation and terrorist acts. These include intelligence sharing, preventing online radicalisation and supporting cooperation between countries. Morocco only does some of these, it is its other policies that cause the problems.

The report also said, 'There has also been a notable shift from hard security measures to a more holistic approach in cooperation with grassroots organisations and frontline practitioners to enhance the resilience of vulnerable communities.'

It then adds, '…although there has been some progress it has been slow. Much more can be done in terms of prevention, the detection of signs of radicalisation, and improving the monitoring and evaluation of programmes and policies. Many challenges remain, such as the return of foreign fighters to Europe and radicalisation in prisons. Moving forward, it is also crucial to determine what 'radicalisation' entails precisely, so that practitioners and policymakers can develop effective counter-narratives that can stop the spread of radical and extremist ideologies.

In the end, there is no simple recipe to prevent radicalisation and the violence stemming from it. The phenomenon is complex, multifaceted, and far-reaching. Our response to it should be equally wide-ranging, comprehensive and multi-layered.'

****

Based on the overwhelming evidence that little has changed, it must mean Morocco has not been sufficiently challenged to identify and then remedy the reasons its citizens have so many terrorist victims' blood on their hands. The previous attacks described in **Villains or Victims? A Global Drug and Terrorism Conundrum,** shows that if its policy makers and rulers had adapted better policies and strategies, few (IF ANY) Moroccans would have been radicalised.

But as the content of the previous chapters illustrate, Morocco has **never** fully addressed the country's poverty issues or applied the right drug policies that are the backbone of its many drug problems. This means the past Moroccan influenced terrorist attacks in France, Spain, Belgium and the UK are unlikely to have happened if it had. This includes Barcelona's which was wholly instigated by men of Moroccan origin.

On the 17th August 2017, TEN Moroccans living in Northern Spain committed the Barcelona and Cambrils terrorist attacks. In the months before, they had been radicalised by the convicted Moroccan drug trafficking imam, Abdelbaki Es Satty, in the town where they lived, Ripoll.

The day before the attack, Es Satty, along with another Moroccan terrorist, died in an explosion at their bomb making factory in Alcanar on the Mediterranean coast of Spain's Catalonia. From records found at the scene, their next targets would have been the Eiffel Tower in Paris and the Sagrada Familiar in Barcelona. These were only thwarted because Es Satty and the terrorists died.

Chapter 9

Barcelona 2017 Terrorist Attacks.
Wake Up Calls from Ripoll and Alcanar.

Of all the towns in all the world, one of the last places the radicalisation of a group of terrorists was likely to happen was Ripoll. This normally peaceful, scenically lovely, twin river town, nestled in the foothills of the Pyrenees in Spain, just an hour from the sea and ski resorts, home to several generations of Moroccans, was about to receive the most agonising wake-up call of all.

When its seemingly well-integrated citizens woke up on 17th August 2017 it was 21°c, at noon it was 32°c, but at 4-50pm the fires of hell broke loose, at that time the temperature rose above the maximum on a gage. No one could have predicted the nightmare that was to unfold before its next dawn.

As reports came in that members of its community had been the perpetrators of the second most deadly terrorist attack in Spain, and one of the most shocking in Europe this century, feelings of anger, shame, sadness, and lack of understanding, that even five years later, still leaves veils of horror, bitterness and disbelief.

From a population of nearly 11,000 people, 5% are of Moroccan origin, at least 10 of whom had been radicalised into terrorism by the convicted drug trafficker, turned imam, Abdelbaki Es Satty.

How this could happen without it being noticed under the noses of their families, work colleagues, friends, and police was and still is a source of amazement. But it did. The consequence resulting in the deaths of 16 people and injuries to 140 in Barcelona, and nearby Cambrils, a popular seaside resort.

How to make sure nothing like it happens anywhere again is a political and social dilemma; it was now the challenge I gave myself.

As such attacks lead to speculation by the media and public as to their reasons, it was important for me to investigate thoroughly before I attempted to disseminate the truth. I am now able to do that based on experience.

After visits to each of the Catalan attack sites, interviews with witnesses and local citizens, visits to the sites of Europe's other Moroccan led terrorist attacks, and by living in Morocco where my single focus was to help put right its drug problems, I am able to describe what I believe is the truth.

In the case of Ripoll, some reasons were obvious as they were the same as the terrorist attacks with which I was familiar in Casablanca, Madrid, Marrakesh, Paris, London, Brussels and New York. So, the sooner I could discover any that were different, the quicker the causes could be highlighted.

As so often is the case where young Moroccans are concerned, experience had taught me to start by looking for issues with drugs. As imam Es Satty had a history of drug trafficking, establishing this link was therefore easy. But as is often the situation with regard to drugs, denial of their use is never far away. It soon seemed this was also the case here.

A clear reason for the perpetrators coming from Ripoll, was the need for better social integration between those practicing Christianity and those who practice Islam. Another was the intellectual and manipulative influences used on the young men who were radicalised by imam Es Satty. And although he died in the explosion in the house used as their bomb factory in Alcanar the day before the Barcelona and Cambrils attacks, it was still his radicalising influence that caused the massacre and shootout.

Normally sleepy
Ripoll

Mosque Ripoll

If everything had gone according to plan, Younes Abouyaaqoub would not have driven a van hitting more than a hundred people walking on Las Ramblas in Barcelona; it was news of the explosion that made him do it.

For months before then, Es Satty and the jihadists from Ripoll had planned to do something far more devastating in Barcelona just a few days later, which accounted for the large amount of bomb making equipment they had been buying and stealing for several months.

One thing is sure, religion is not to blame - though far too often that is where blame is placed. Anyone who understands the teachings of Islam and Christianity knows that on the subjects of love and murder, they contain very few differences.

Islam teaches that God is so loving that He created His attribute of love as an instinct in us. Therefore, it is a Muslim's duty to love one another as God loves us. In the Qur'an it states, 'If you kill one person, it is as if you kill the whole of humanity. If you save one person, it will be as if you save the whole of humanity'.

Christianity teaches much the same, love they neighbour as thyself, do unto others as you would be done by. Love is patient, love is kind. It does not envy, it does not boast, it is not proud. It does not dishonour others, it is not self-seeking, it is not easily angered, it keeps no record of wrongs. Love does not delight in evil but rejoices with the truth. It always protects, always trusts, always hopes, and always perseveres.

As the Ten Commandments are applicable to both Islam and Christianity, (and Judaism), this cannot be refuted. The Bible's 6th Commandment states, 'Thou Shall Not Murder or Kill'.

In other words, acts of love are fundamental to each of these religions; so, murder, and therefore terrorism, are not and never could be acts of God.

This leaves the question, what were the real reasons for the Catalan attacks and what can be done to prevent more happening?

Although I believe I have discovered the answers, getting them put into practice by those who can change laws and policies in Morocco may not be easy.

After the initial rampage on Las Ramblas, the perpetrator, Younes Abouyaaqoub abandoned the van and fled on foot. He then murdered another person to steal their car and flee the area.

Hours later, five other members of the Ripoll terrorist cell carried out a second attack in the nearby town of Cambrils. Several pedestrians were knocked down by their vehicle and a woman was stabbed to death. The six perpetrators were all later shot dead by police, while imam Es Satty and another terrorist had died the day before when their bomb factory in Alcanar exploded.

The Alcanar house had more than 120 gas canisters inside, which police believe the cell was attempting to make into one large bomb, or three smaller bombs to be placed in three vans they had rented. It was these that were accidentally detonated on 16th August. Three more men were also arrested by Spanish authorities and later convicted.

La Rambla
Barcelona

Van used in
massacre.

Joan Miró commemorative plaque on Las Ramblas where the van driven by Younes Abouyaaqoub stopped before he fled into a nearby market.

At around 21:30 the same day, Houssaine Abouyaaqoub, Omar Hichamy, Mohamed Hichamy, Moussa Oukabir, and Said Aalla were seen on a security camera purchasing four knives and an axe. Two and a half hours later, these men drove an automobile into a crowd of pedestrians before it rolled over at a crossroads in Cambrils. The five individuals inside were wearing fake suicide vests and attacked bystanders with knives. They stabbed a 63-year-old Spanish woman to death, and injured six other people in the attack, including a Cuban tourist and a police officer.

A police officer shot and killed four of the assailants, while a fifth died of his injuries later. It did not take long for the police to realise these men were part of the same terrorist cell that caused the Barcelona attack hours earlier.

Memorial site of terrorist deaths in Cambrils after Barcelona attacks.

The day prior to the Barcelona attacks, an explosion destroyed the terrorists bomb factory in their Alcanar hideout, where imam Abdelbaki Es Satty and terrorist, Youssef Aallaa died. Initially, police thought it was a gas explosion, but soon realised it was caused by explosives going off accidentally. A Moroccan man was injured and taken to hospital. Later, his questioning helped piece together what turned out to be random attacks.

The explosive TATP and 120 canisters of butane and propane were found inside the Alcanar property. It was only later the police discovered the terrorists intended to take vans loaded with them to Barcelona to carry out the originally planned attacks, which would have been devastating. Police chief Josep Lluís Trapero said he believed the terrorists were in the process of manipulating the gas canisters when they exploded. It was only after that those alive decided to conduct the vehicle ramming attacks instead.

How Es Satty was able to practice as an imam is a mystery. His criminal record meant he had his phone tapped, had two smuggling convictions, and spent four years in prison. Yet, he lived under the radar while he organized the deadliest terrorist attack in Spain since the 2004 Madrid train bombings.

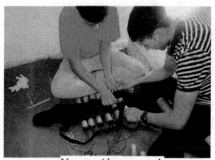
Younes Abouyaaqoub
and Youssef

Es Satty had a criminal
record for years

Aalla preparing explosives in Alcanar.

House in Alcanar used as bomb factory accidently destroyed where imam died.

Four days later, police were tipped off as to Abouyaaqoub's whereabouts: Subirats, a small town 30 miles outside Barcelona. Police said that when they found him, he was wearing an explosive belt. They shot him dead, while the explosive belt turned out to be fake. He is said to have shouted; 'Allahu akbar' – 'God is most great' before being killed.

Within a week, eight suspected members of the cell behind the attack were dead, and four were in police custody in Spain. Two more suspects were detained in Morocco. The police response it was claimed it was a success.

At first, it looked good for the Catalan police, the Mossos D'Esquadra, who operate separately from Spain's national and paramilitary police forces. The political climate was hot as Catalonia was just six weeks away from a referendum on independence. But the Madrid government had declared this illegal, while most of the Catalan government was determined to carry it through. The Spanish and Catalan press were each eager to paint the attack on Barcelona as the failure of the other's police. As more and more information emerged, the picture got murkier and murkier.

Chapter 10

9/11 and the Iraq War.

On September 11, 2001 (9/11), 19 militants from the Islamic extremist group al Qaeda hijacked four airplanes and carried out suicide attacks against targets in America. Two planes were flown into the twin towers of the World Trade Centre in New York City, a third hit the Pentagon in Arlington, Virginia, near Washington, D.C., and the fourth crashed in a field in Pennsylvania.

Nearly 3,000 people died during the attacks, including 19 hijackers, with many injured. The effects shocked not just Americans but the rest of the world, initiating much anger and some reflection. Unfortunately, the former triggered an eye-for-an-eye retaliation by the US government with a country that had not caused the attacks.

Today many believe the Islamophobic nature of this seemingly bullying, disproportionate, misguided, possibly illegal response by the American, British, Spanish and Portuguese governments caused resentment among extremists who responded by carrying out the series of terrorist attacks that followed in Europe and North Africa, the majority of which were by Moroccans.

The Iraq war began in 2003 and continued to 2011; though its aftermath has continued, leaving much instability and bloodshed in a country that always had deep divides. Official estimates are that at least 400,000 died.

These results make it appear that the American, British, and Spanish protagonists had not taken this into account when they led the invasion to overthrow the Iraqi government and Saddam Hussein. As this was already amid global controversy - especially in these three countries - because the weapons inspectors had not found any weapons of mass destruction and was before they were allowed to complete their surveys, this lack of understanding has caused deep consternation.

Many people claimed the attack was a criminal act. This was substantiated when the United Nations Secretary-General Kofi Annan said: "From our point of view and the UN Charter point of view, it [the war] was illegal." As Gandhi said, 'an eye for an eye makes the whole world blind.'

The invasion of Iraq was also strongly opposed by some long-standing U.S. allies, including the governments of France, Germany, and New Zealand. Their leaders argued that there was no evidence of weapons of mass destruction in Iraq and that invading that country was not justified in the context of UNMOVIC's 12 February 2003 report. About 5,000 chemical warheads, shells or aviation bombs were discovered during the Iraq War, but these had been abandoned earlier.

On 15 February 2003, a month before the invasion, there were worldwide protests against the war, including a rally of three million people in Rome, which is the largest-ever anti-war rally. In total it is estimated around 36 million people across the globe took part in almost 3,000 protests against the Iraq war. *As with the failed war on drugs, will politicians ever learn?*

Twin Tower Attacks

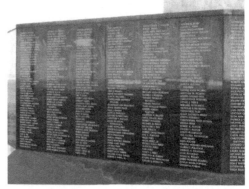

Twin Tower memorials

Although the 9/11 attack was believed to be masterminded by Osama bin laden, he was hugely helped by four men known as the Hamburg Cell because they spoke English. They, in turn, were influenced by the Moroccan imam, Zacarias Moussaoui, who was known as "the cells' spiritual father" who helped execute the 9/11 attacks. Moussaoui had founded the Salafiya Jihadiya, Reformist Holy War

Jihadists, movement. He was tried in the United States as the '20th hijacker' for 9/11.

Another perpetrator of the 11 September 2001 terror attacks on the United States, was also Moroccan. He was the only person convicted of the attacks, and before he was deported back to Morocco, had spent almost 15 years in prison for his part in the deaths of passengers aboard the highjacked aeroplanes used in the attacks.

Mounir el-Motassadeq was born in Marrakech on April 3, 1974. He was convicted by a German court of being a member of al-Qaeda and of assisting the hijackers in the September 11 attacks. On 15 October 2018, el-Motassadeq was deported to Morocco after serving his sentence.

Motassadeq went to Germany in 1993 and moved to Hamburg in 1995, where he studied electrical engineering at the Hamburg University of Technology. While there he moved into an apartment owned by fellow student, Mohamed Atta and lived there with several other people who would later be accused by the U.S. and German authorities of leading the September 11, 2001, attacks.

In court it was claimed, Motassadeq was not only a friend of suicide bomber and mastermind of the attacks, Mohamed Atta, but his other friends included two more suicide bombers, Marwan al-Shehhi and Ziad Jarrah, who were all part of the "Hamburg cell".

Motassadeq maintained his innocence during his 2006 trial. He claimed he had merely been a close friend of the men, but the court decided he had helped the 'cell' with the logistics of planning their attacks, as well as keeping up rental payments once they had left for the US, to maintain the appearance that they were planning to return.

Part 2

Chapter 11

Organised Crime

Originally the term 'mafia' referred to the organised crime committed by societies of criminals of primarily Italian or Sicilian birth or extraction. Many historians believe that it emerged in Sicily in the 19th century during Italy's unification, but others suggest it originated during the late Middle Ages, possibly as a secret organization dedicated to overthrowing the rule of the various foreign conquerors of the island, especially from Spain, Arabia, and France of Scandinavian descent.

The mafia name owed its origin to and drew its members from the many small private armies that were hired by absentee landlords to protect their landed estates from bandits in the lawless conditions that prevailed over much of Sicily through the centuries.

During the 18th and 19th centuries, the energetic ruffians in these private armies organized themselves and grew so powerful that they turned against the landowners and became the sole law on many of the estates, extorting money from the landowners in return for protecting the latter's crops.

The diaspora of Italians meant an American mafia came to power in the 1920s prohibition era after the earlier success of its bootleg liquor business. By the 1950s, it had become the preeminent organized-crime network in North America. Like the Sicilian mafia, American mafia families aimed to be as anonymous as possible, as their influence spreads to bribing and intimidating public officials, business leaders, witnesses, and juries.

Today there are organised crime mafias in many countries. The best known are the Italian, Japanese Yakuza – believed to be the largest –, Russian, Albanian – most ruthless -, Mexican, Israeli, Chinese triads, Columbian drug cartels, and over 100 separate organisations spread around the world.

The most notorious commodities associated with organised crime are illegal drugs. The United Nations Office on Drugs and Crime (UNODC) estimates the global value is $32 billion US dollars.

The Mocro-Maffia is the name given to criminal organisations that are mainly composed of people of Moroccan descent in the Netherlands and Belgium. They are renowned for trafficking large quantities of drugs through France, Spain, Portugal, the Netherlands, and Belgium, from where they are distributed to the rest of Europe. Their criminal activities also include human and arms trafficking, as well as contraband such as cigarettes and alcohol.

It is big business. In 2017, the US State Department estimated that the export of cannabis and its by-products represent 23% of Morocco's Gross Domestic Product (GDP). If this is correct, in 2022 it represented $32.8 billion. Many believe the financial beneficiaries are not just in Europe, they include high-ranking members of the Moroccan police and leading dignitaries in that country's government.

The most obvious people taking advantage of this are the Moroccan criminal networks which have been active in Europe since the 1990s. A consequence is that since 2012 Dutch and Belgian Moroccan gangs have been at war over drug distribution across the Netherlands and Belgium. As a result, many involved have been killed - at least 100. According to Interpol, Antwerp and Amsterdam have become the epicenters for Europe's illicit drug trade. This has led to an increase in crime, including murder, shootings, bombings, arson, kidnappings, torture, and intimidation.

To combat the trade, Interpol says more needs to be done to tackle production at source and target corruption at ports.

But this is not the answer. It shows a lack of understanding of the reasons people take drugs and why the world's drug laws, and past policies have not and will never work.

The Dutch and Belgian mafias are big but the biggest in Europe is Italy's 'Ndrangheta, and because of rich pickings, it has also established a presence in the Benelux countries. This included buying properties in a single neighbourhood in Brussels, from which they laundered money originating from drug trafficking. In 2004, 47 people were arrested, accused of drug trafficking and money laundering in order to purchase real estate in Brussels totalling 28,000,000 euros.

Their activities spread to the Netherlands. There, large quantities of heroin and cocaine were purchased by rival mafias from Sicily, the Pesce-Bellocco and Strangia. As members of these were involved in gun wars, it was not surprising gang killings rife in Italy's homeland mafias, escalated elsewhere.

This was evidenced in the Duisburg massacre in Germany when two gunmen killed six men, believed to be because of a long-running feud between 'Ndranggheta clans from Sicily with strong ties to Amsterdam. While, two members of the group reportedly killed a man in Marrakech with links to drug trafficking. The group is also suspected of being linked to the murder of the son of a Moroccan judge.

Derk Wiersum, an Amsterdam lawyer specialising in organised crime and drug trafficking networks, and as well as Peter R. de Vries, the investigative journalist who reported on drug trafficking, were assassinated in 2019 and 2021 respectively, allegedly by the Mocro-Maffia. A Belgian girl of Moroccan origin, aged 11, was killed when her parents' home was shot at – allegedly by the group.

In September 2021, an alert was raised by Dutch security services, who believed that Prime Minister Mark Rutte was under threat from members of the

Mocro-Maffia. Likewise, Dutch Crown Princess Catharina-Amalia is protected by heavy security following rumours of kidnapping threats reportedly linked to the group.

By 2023, the ranking of Europe's links to Latin American cocaine meant Belgium and the Netherlands had overtaken Spain as the main entry points for this confidence-enhancing drug. The 65.6 tonnes of it intercepted at the port of Antwerp in 2020 had nearly doubled by 2022. Moroccan mafias being the key link.

When the Netherlands opened its cannabis market in the 1970s, Dutch and Belgian nationals of Moroccan descent took advantage of their close family links with cannabis growers in the northern mountains of Morocco's Rif region. What started as the trafficking of the much sought-after hashish, slowly extended to cocaine, a more lucratively traded drug.

Today's powerful Mocro-Maffia drug cartel emerged from this trade in the 1990s, controlling a third of Europe's cocaine market, and working mainly from the Netherlands and Belgium.

Since then, Latin American drug traffickers have increasingly used Morocco and other Maghreb countries, as well as those based in Europe, like the Mocro-Maffia, in their transnational cocaine trade.

To transport the drugs, Colombian and Mexican cartels used established drug routes from North Africa to Spain via the Mediterranean coast city of Algeciras, after which Spanish traffickers took them to its north Atlantic coast. Today, the 'Mocro-Maffia' is a serious threat to both the European Union and Africa

But this became increasingly risky, as Moroccan, and Spanish authorities tightened their border controls and search operations. So, traffickers are now using Belgium and the Netherlands as their preferred ports. The huge size of containers and amount of traffic their ports accommodate makes it difficult for authorities to address the problem.

In the 2021, Rotterdam port authorities report it highlighted that '... crime is high on our agenda, tackling it is a challenge facing society as a whole ... We do not want criminals to use the port for nefarious ends. We are working with various agencies in the port to maintain security and combat drugs-related crime.'

It seems corruption is a major issue in the enabling of cocaine trafficking from Latin America to Rotterdam and Antwerp via Africa. So, for Mexican and South American drug cartels, the Mocro-Maffia's ability to corrupt those in authority in transit countries makes them essential allies.

Intercepted audio exchanges have revealed how Mocro-Maffia members boast about bribing customs officers in the Port of Dakar (Senegal, West Africa), which is used as a transit point. Likewise, dockers in Antwerp and Rotterdam are being paid up to €100,000 to relocate containers to avoid police and customs control.

In the meantime, the Netherlands remains an ideal place for drug traffickers to invest their money, as along with Belgium, it is a money laundering haven. Antwerp, the world capital of diamond processing, is a destination for *washing* drug proceeds, while the real estate sector in Belgium serves as a primary route for money laundering.

In the Netherlands, a reported €16 billion is laundered annually due to its large, international and digitised financial sector; plus, the creation of shell companies has made money laundering easy there.

One reason for the Mocro-Maffia's success in the Netherlands is that disorganised public authorities are faced with organised criminality, says Hans Werdmölder, author of Netherlands a Narco-State.

To deal with this, some suggest the authorities and law enforcement must introduce measures to counter this threat. Modern surveillance equipment such as drones, mobile scanners and robots are lacking in the Netherlands, Belgium, and Morocco. Installing or modernising such equipment and training law enforcement to use these tools effectively could help detect more drugs at the transit hubs in Morocco and the Rotterdam and Antwerp ports.

But others recommend a different approach, believing the authorities should change their mindset about drugs. Rather than focusing on stopping the drug trade, measures should be taken to curb the associated violence. In the 1980's Italy introduced new legislation and judicial measures that meant violence related to drug trafficking lessened.

Instead of judicial condemnation, Italian authorities punish drug traffickers financially, targeting their assets. Around $6 billion in cash and assets are confiscated from drug traffickers annually in Italy, which is redistributed to non-governmental organisations. Another aim is to show citizens and international critics that Italy has taken measures with positive results in its fight against drug traffickers and the mafia.

By the 21st Century, the Mocro-Maffia had become a serious threat to the European Union and Africa. In a relatively short time, the organisation became a major trafficking group in Europe. Its links with organised criminal groups in Morocco and Latin America making it a persistent and growing threat in many countries on both continents.

The Moroccan mafia does not, however, include Moroccan Jewish crime families such as the Abergil crime family as well as the Abutbul and Domrani clans, who are rather considered to be a part of the Israeli mafia. That said, Moroccan - Israeli mafia clans are known for having collaborated closely together with the Mocro-Maffia in the Netherlands and Belgium, especially in the worldwide distribution of synthetic drugs such as MDMA. This is mostly due to the fact that the Netherlands is the largest producer of MDMA and amphetamines in the world.

The Netherlands

Two of the Netherlands' drug gang ringleaders were Samir Bouyakhrichan and Houssaine Ait Soussan. Bouyakhrichan was a Moroccan billionaire drug trafficker and the richest Amsterdam drug lord of the 2000s. The Dutch media considered him to be one of the biggest traffickers the continent ever had, controlling the shipment of drugs all over Europe. Competing with him was Ridouan Taghi's Mocro-Maffia murderous organization, which led to him being assassinated in a restaurant in Marbella in 2014.

Soussan is a criminal born in Amsterdam of Moroccan origin, a large scale drug trafficker, and notable figure in the Mocro-Maffia in both the Netherlands and Belgium. He is reputed to have distributed tons of cocaine and for years was wanted by Interpol for his involvement in assassinations and kidnappings, the majority of which took place in Antwerp and Brussels.

Notorious criminals of Moroccan origin have been assassinated in the Benelux Mocro-Maffia gang wars. These include Najeb Bouhbouh and Benauouf Adanami, while many such as Najib Himmich, Naoufal Fassih, Mustapha El Fechtali and Said Razzouki attained notoriety for smuggling cocaine, cannabis, and synthetic drugs.

In addition to north Moroccan links to the port of Algeciras on Spain's Mediterranean coast, they have relationships with Colombian and Mexican cartels using the ports of Rotterdam in the Netherlands and Antwerp in Belgium to traffic drugs all over Europe.

Cocaine seized in Rotterdam.

Although the 2018 Dutch TV series, *Mocro-Maffia* brought attention to the criminal activities of the Moroccan mafia in the Netherlands, it was the murder of the investigative journalist, Peter R. de Vries on 6th July 2021, in Amsterdam that brought it to global attention. As this followed the murders of two prosecution witnesses in the Moroccan Ridouan Taghi's trial, the Dutch are afraid the Netherlands will become classified as a 'Narco-State.'

Mr de Vries had won critical acclaim for his reporting on the Dutch underworld, including the kidnapping of Freddy Heineken - the brewing millionaire. But it was while he was advising Nabil Bakkali, a former Mocro-Maffia gang member acting as a witness against alleged Moroccan drug lord Ridouan Taghi that it is assumed caused his murder.

Prosecutors believe Mr. De Vries was killed on the orders of Taghi, who is on trial for being the head of a gang that planned a string of underworld assassinations between 2015 and 2017, as well as drug trafficking. He and sixteen others are accused of carrying out six murders and planning another seven over an 18-month period.

However, the execution of Mr de Vries backfired on the perpetrators as it caused global condemnation. International newspapers exposed the criminal activities of everyone associated with Taghi as well as causing even more hatred to those involved in the illicit drug trade.

Tributes to Peter R de Vries where he was murdered.

Many blame the Netherlands' drug problems on the hypocritical way it deals with cannabis. This is because it is illegal to produce it there, but it is legal to sell it in designated Coffee Shops. How can this be allowed is the question?

The result of the Netherlands' confusing laws seems to have helped create its huge underground business, which has diversified not just into cocaine but also into crystal meth. Today it is believed the Dutch are the biggest producers in Europe; with regard to ecstasy, they lead the world.

Amsterdam Coffee Shop Cannabis menus.

In addition, the Netherlands' confusing laws seems to have helped create its huge underground drug business, which diversified not just into cocaine but also into crystal meths. By 2014, it was believed the Dutch were the biggest producers in Europe, and regarding ecstasy, they led the world. And it was this that caused the creation of Dutch mafias that led to the bloody war between gangs over a missing €15 million cocaine shipment, which claimed at least fourteen lives spread across Europe.

According to the Dutch justice ministry, which investigated the murders, the gang's origin stemmed from a stolen batch of cocaine in 2012. It is believed the estimated 200 tonnes came through Antwerp, and was bound for the UK and Ireland, where it would sell at €50,000 a kilo compared to €30,000 in Netherlands.

In March 2012, Antwerp customs had seized 200 kilos of cocaine. Unknown to them, although it was a massive seizure, it was but part of a much bigger load. They later came to believe it was part of a much larger consignment that had been stolen and was turning up in small quantities of kilos, selling for lower than usual prices.

Investigators now believe a Dutch gang calling themselves the Turtles stole part of the consignment from a rival gang. Dutch journalist and author of Mocro-Maffia, Wouter Laumans, said at the time: "The seizure in Antwerp was not reported in the media until recently, so the gang thought all of it had been ripped. Then all hell has been let loose. There is no doubt in my mind that a lot of this cocaine was on its way to the UK where they can get a higher price for it. These guys are working with the British without a doubt. It's like some kind of Guy Ritchie film, except it's not funny."

A second British link to the victims emerged when Samir Bouyakhrichan, a major figure in the Dutch Moroccan underworld, was shot dead. Several revenge killings followed, including the Brazilian girlfriend of a Dutch criminal, who had been accused of luring another criminal to his death.

The number and breadth of the shootings shocked the Dutch public because of their brazen quality, violence, and brutally. Automatic weapons were used in several incidents, while in one failed assassination attempt in an Amsterdam café, bystanders were badly injured.

The stolen cocaine death toll - October 2012 to September 2014.

18 October 2012: Najeb Bouhbouh, (Moroccan) 34, gunned down outside the Crowne Plaza Hotel in Antwerp

29 December 2012: Youseff Lkhorf and Said El Yazidi, (Moroccans) shot dead in a shootout in Amsterdam in which gang boss Benaouf Adaoui, (Moroccan), the Netherlands most dangerous drug lord survived. Police were also shot at.

16 March 2013: Rida Bennajem (Moroccan), shot dead in Amsterdam. Believed to be one of the hitmen involved in murder of Najeb Bouhbouh

26 May 2013: Souhail Laachir, (Moroccan), shot dead Amsterdam. He was involved in the finances of Benaouf Adaoui.

24 August 2013: Chris Bouman, 36, involved in luring Najeb Bouhbouh to the Crowne Plaza, committed suicide in prison awaiting charges on October 18, 2012, murder. Police believe he had been threatened while in custody.

20 February 2014: Alexander Gillis,30, friend of Gwenette Martha shot dead Amsterdam.

22 March 2014: Mohammed El Mayouri, 30, a hitman for the Benaouf group shot dead Amsterdam.

22 May 2014: Gwenette Martha, best friend of Najeb Bouhbouh, shot dead Amsterdam.

13 July 2014: Stefan Eggermont shot dead in case of mistaken identity. Investigators believed that the shooters were targeting Omar Lkhorf brother of

Youseff Lkhorf killed in December 2012. Omar Lkhorf drove the same car as Stefan, often parked in a similar spot and lived nearby.

16 August 2014: Derkiaoui Van Der Meijden, 34, shot dead Amsterdam. Associate of Gwenette Martha and hit man believed to be involved in the December 29, 2012, shootings. Wearing a bullet proof vest, he was gunned down by two men brandishing AK 47's

28 August 2014: Samir Bouyakhrichan, 36, head of another organised crime group and friend of Benaouf group shot dead Marbella, Spain

3 September 2014: Massod Amin Hosseini, 30 shot dead Amsterdam. Massod was known on the periphery of both groups.

****

Belgium

In the Netherlands, everyone knows of the 'Mocro-mafia', its criminal gangs of Moroccan origin. And just as it drips in Brussels when it rains in Paris, Amsterdam and Antwerp have become equally intertwined.

This Flemish city on the river Scheldt estuary is important for the Mocro-mafia as it uses its port to import drugs from South America and Africa. To service this, it set up a branch in the Borgerhout district of Antwerp, staffed by Moroccan families. They started as 'snatchers', who, at the request of Dutch drug lords, stole cocaine from incoming shipments. But soon the drug snatchers realised they would be better off acting alone. Today they are known as the 'Borgerokko mafia' and act independently. This part of Antwerp now being called 'Coke City'.

In December 2022, the Belgian justice minister, Vincent Van Quickenborne said, 'the international drug mafia now poses as big a threat to national security as the Islamic State terrorists who bombed Brussels six years ago'.

On 10th January 2023, the mayor of Antwerp, Bart De Wever said, "What I feared for a long time has happened: an innocent victim has fallen." He was responding to the drive-by killing of an 11-year-old girl, Firdaous El J, whose family is linked to Moroccan cocaine gangs in Antwerp. He added, "The national drug plan is frankly a disappointment."

The motive behind the shooting is believed to have been a "settling of scores" between rival gangs of the "Mocro Mafia", drawn from the Moroccan communities in the Netherlands and Belgium. One of the girl's relatives is believed to be Younes El Ballouti, known as "El Magico", a declared fugitive and cocaine smuggler. In 2017, police say he was kidnapped by mafia rivals and released on payment of €5 million.

Antwerp in Belgium claims to have the biggest port area by size in the world, approximately 130 square kilometers occupying both sides of the river Scheldt as it flows into the North Sea. It is the second largest by freight size after Rotterdam in Europe. It is the biggest port for smuggling cocaine to the rest of the continent, with Rotterdam not far behind. Just 100 kilometres in distance apart, these two cities have become the main ports of entrance for drugs into Europe.

Antwerp's network is connected to the interior by rail, road, rivers and canals, providing a mix of transportation alternatives. As traffickers are renowned for finding innovative ways to ship drugs, and as there are not enough officials to check every ships' cargo, it is estimated at least 90% reach their designated destinations.

In 2022, over 100 tonnes of cocaine were seized in Belgium —more than in any other country in the EU, while an estimated 1,000 tonnes reaches the city's port in a year - smuggled inside anything from crates of bananas to containers of pet food.

On 21st September 2022, an article in Le Monde, the French newspaper, read, 'Narco-state' fears in Belgium after summer of violence. With the following November's court case relating to the bomb attacks in Brussels in 2017, it could have read, '...after *years* of violence.' It could have also added, the words 'drug related', as this applied to both.

In the same article it said, 'It all started in 2012, when Dutch traffickers kidnapped one of the members of a family who had tried to steal a batch of cocaine offloaded from a container at the port of Antwerp. The family relented when they received a photo of the meat grinder the kidnappers were threatening to feed the young man into.' It goes on to describe how this summer there have been shootings, attempted arson, stabbings and grenade attacks in Brussels and Antwerp.

This has led to the formation of a special police unit to deal with the drug gangs in Antwerp as the street value of the drugs that pass through its port is up to $60 billion. The knock-on effect was over 80 acts of violence were committed in Antwerp. Today, those arrested and convicted, fill a whole wing of Antwerp prison.

But with so much money involved in the legal and illegal drug markets, it is a better understanding and different strategies that are needed.

Experience shows that the police, politicians, and the pharmaceutical industry are not the best suited authorities to do this. Specialist teams of men and women without personal agendas or preconceived ideas are needed to apply the solutions that are needed.

Chapter 12

A Solution to Global and Morocco's Drug Problems

With so much money involved, it was inevitable the drug industry would attract some unscrupulous personnel to manufacture, grow and distribute its many legal and illegal products. As this includes pharmaceutical firms and brewers, as well as illicit drugs, to address regulation issues it is important to consider every factor. Once that is done, just as physicians first diagnosis then prescribe for an illness, so could the best remedies be applied to resolve the many problems currently caused by mood altering addictive drugs.

People take legal drugs to alter their mood. Whether it is alcohol to celebrate winning the lottery, put life into a party, give courage to an airline passenger afraid of a plane crash, lessen the pain of losing a loved one, or tranquillisers to combat anxiety, sleeping pills to help insomniacs, anti-depressants to combat depression or opiates to deaden pain, it is always for the effect.

This is the same for illegal drugs and in most instances they are no more addictive.

Cannabis makes users feel high, cocaine is a stimulant, heroin can have a euphoric effect, magic mushrooms are hallucinatory, and so on.

Putting all I knew together, including my experience as a business development adviser to the pharmaceutical industry, I examined the global situation regarding other killer diseases and their treatment. As it was topical and there was an obvious similarity, the place to start was Covid-19.

Since it was declared a pandemic by the WHO in March 2020, more than 6.5 million people have died from Covid-19. In the same period, approximately the same number died from drug addiction and alcoholism. But while Covid-19 deaths only go back to Dec 2019; the annual death rate for drugs and alcohol goes back hundreds of years.

So why had there been such a furore about Covid-19, yet a comparative complacency regarding drug and alcohol deaths? My first thought was: is money the cause?

An initial review guided me where to begin. The industries involved in slavery to drugs included some of the biggest on the planet; pharmaceutical, brewing and tobacco. Each has firms who make mountains of money from drugs and related addictions; meaning free permanent recovery from diseases linked to their drugs would not be in their best financial interest.

But the disease of Covid-19 was different. Developing a drug that treated it would not only make the firms that create it a lot of money, but it would also give them credibility - something the pharmaceutical industry had lost in recent years.

Lawsuits totalling more than US$30 billion exposes this issue, which includes some of the biggest firms in the industry.

The panic driven urgency to develop a treatment for Covid-19 took almost a year and cost billions of dollars, while research is still going on as new variations of the disease develop. Whereas a successful free treatment for alcoholism has been available for over eighty years, and although it has helped 3,500,000 million alcoholics recover in 175 countries in 80 languages, it is hard to believe that many in the medical profession still do not offer it as the No. 1 treatment.

What is more, because of AA's success, people with other addictions started new fellowships that replicate its 12-Steps of recovery programme as they realised that with only a slight adaptation, the same programme would work for them.

This begged three questions:

Why had not Big Pharma's executives made sure their medical representatives told the medical profession?

Why are these programmes not available everywhere for everyone who needs them?

Why are there still countries and members of the medical profession who do not propose a treatment that works for every drug addict who applies its principles?

The facts and examples in this book were originally aimed at exposing Morocco's links to terrorism and organised crime, mostly because of its hypocritical drug laws and wayward addiction treatment policies. However, Morocco is not alone with this, and although many of its problems are self-inflicted, some are the result of other countries' laws and regimes, especially America's. And it is these irresponsible policies that are at the heart of many of the world's drug problems.

By publishing this book, it is hoped that because of the horrendous consequences, countries that have wayward and hypocritical drug laws will change them and replace ineffective treatment of drug addiction and alcoholism with methods that work. And because not all the world's doctors and psychiatrists are aware of NA and AA's success, *this applies to almost every country in the world.*

What would help make the changes happen is for the United Nations and World Health Organisation to give their full support to the world's most effective drug policies and addiction treatments. If they make statements to this effect, any country whose politicians and medical profession do not comply with what is best would be exposed in the same way as Morocco.

Reflecting on my thirty-five years' experience as a business development adviser to the pharmaceutical industry and the successful creation of Covid-19 treatment vaccines by *several firms,* it was clear a united effort to develop one would have been better. Expanding this idea, it is obvious it would be the same for any disease, so applying what is already known to work to solve drug problems and treat addiction must be better too.

With all the facts put together, it was obvious that a co-ordinated combined approach would help other difficult issues: a formular that could include problems such as poverty, food and water supplies. Whereas in 2022, it was easy to see how the opposite scenario had been applied. It meant Russia was able to block supplies of oil and gas to many countries. This caused shortages which initiated a cost-of-living crises and more poverty.

So, the question is, why are such approaches not applied?

Again, the answer is money and the misplaced power it gives a minority of people. And this being deeply imbedded in society, means it could take centuries to make the essential changes, as it will face greed-based opposition from the individuals whose wealth or positions have given them far too much ruling power.

However, if Morocco were to admit the wrongness of its past regime and introduces new policies that have proved to be better in other countries, it would be applauded. And as King Mohamed VIth has the financial and political power to do this, and he is serious that his aim is to improve Morocco's poor image with regard to drugs and poverty, putting such policies into practice would be a good place for him to start. By sharing his riches and refraining from past self-serving materialistic habits, it would also give him and the country he presides over, credibility.

But this is unlikely to happen unless there are enough internal and external pressures put on Morocco's king. In his 24 years reign, the key issues that cause the country's problems have not been changed. In the 2023, United Nation's Sustainable Development Solutions Network's, 'World Happiness Report', Morocco was ranked 100 out of 109, lower than all the other Arabic countries, even worse than war-ravaged Iraq, and Palestine.

This unbiased report is based on a global survey from people in more than 150 countries. The ranking reflects data on average life evaluations over a period of three years: the 2023 ranking covering 2020 to 2022.

To measure average life evaluations, the report tracks six factors: income, health, having someone to count on, having a sense of freedom to make key life decisions, generosity, and the absence of corruption. In Morocco's case each of the six factors play big roles in supporting its low life evaluations.

On the other hand, to most visitors, Morocco's natural beauty and other attractions enable it to get away with portraying a positive image. Thanks to alluring marketing, and people who only see its beautiful Mediterranean and Atlantic coasts, magnificent mountains, and deserts, sample its delicious cuisine, stay in sumptuous Riads, and shop in its excellent markets, the inhumane tragedies of daily life there are seldom witnessed; except that is by the victims. Which is also the case of the organised crime and other horrific effects caused by its drug policies.

One of the most appalling aspects of Morocco's Mr Hyde character is the daily plight of its 'cargo women'. Embedded in the north Moroccan coast, the Spanish enclaves of Ceuta and Melilla represent Europe's southernmost border. There is no formal customs agreement between these two autonomous cities and Morocco, and this has given rise to a system where goods are smuggled across the border as 'personal luggage' to avoid customs charges and taxes.

The burden of this work falls on Moroccan "cargo women", who carry huge bales of goods on their backs over the border. These women, without contracts, social security, or healthcare, suffer abuse and harassment at the hands of the border police. They earn a pittance, while the Spanish cities of Ceuta and Melilla earn over €400 million euros from their labour.

Worse still, the extreme poverty in north Morocco means the desperate people who do this are casualties of occasional stampedes. Women have died because of this abdominal situation, yet it still happens every day.

This is one of many atrocities that contribute to the low self-esteem of Moroccans. They are ware such issues exist, whereas very few outsiders know, because this part of the country is so poor few foreigners visit there. So, as much as possible, along with the sight of its drug addicted street children, such eyesores and inhumane issues, Morocco's authorities sweep under the carpet.

Women carrying cargo at Ceuta Morocco-Spanish border.

At least as horrendous and damaging to Morocco's image at home, and abroad, was the case of the fishermen, Mouhcine Fikri. After catching swordfish to pay for food for his extremely poor family in El Hoceima, North Morocco, his catch of fish was confiscated by the police. After they disposed of them in a refuse truck, Mr. Fikri's desperation meant he climbed into the truck to try to retrieve them and was mangled to death.

The horror of the incident led to demonstrations across Morocco, reminding people of the vendor in Tunisia who set himself on fire that started the Arab Spring.

Demonstrations spread across Morocco when a fisherman died trying to rescue his catch from a refuse truck after they were confiscated by police.

If Morocco's king and Government applied the measures that would get rid of poverty and the country's many drug problems, more foreign businesses should want to establish themselves here, while more tourists would also visit. As a result, such actions could propagate other countries to do the same. And if that were to happen, in time, King Mohamed VIth may even be nominated for the Nobel Peace Prize.

But now, it is unlikely, so, there will be more of the same until such poor governance leads to another Moroccan influenced terrorist attack. And when that happens (not if!), the contents of this book should be used to highlight the negligence, not only of Morocco's king and government, but politicians, the pharmaceutical industry, and some people in the medical profession globally.

If such reverses of policies are postponed, or not rightly applied, those responsible will have failed in their duties, and their apathetic omissions will call forth the condemnation of all far-sighted citizens and those victims who follow. One more such tragedy would be to many, but a lot more will be likely.

****

A Better Alternative.

As a starting point, there is an approach to tackling drug problems that would guarantee better results regarding the criminal consequences associated with drug taking. That would also lower the need for policing and border controls; in time it should eliminate them.

As many of the recipients of illegal drugs will be addicts, they will be behind some of the most heinous crimes. So, it is essential to deal with their disease at its root cause. When that is done, the organised crime and terrorist attacks committed by such desperate or radicalised drug addicts would stop. *only **total abstinence** is*.

For this to happen, *harm reduction is categorically not the answer,* and for this to be applied, it needs every medical professional who treats drug addicts and alcoholics to guide sufferers to the appropriate treatment to conquer their disease.

Sadly, at this time in May 2023, only a small percentage of doctors, psychiatrists and psychoanalysts do that, and in Morocco there are virtually none.

Chapter 13

Thwarted Terrorist Attacks

Thalys Train Attack. On 21 August 2015, a **Moroccan** man, Ayoub El Khazzani, opened fire on a Thalys high speed train on its way from Amsterdam to Paris. Four people were injured, including the assailant. In this instance passengers who were later rewarded for their bravery were able to subdue him.

The train had just crossed the border from Belgium into France when the attack occurred at 17-45. The terrorist had gone to a toilet in carriage number 12 to remove his shirt. Wearing a knapsack containing eight loaded magazines, a 9mm luger pistol, knife and carrying a bottle of gasoline, he emerged brandishing a Draco carbine with a 30-round magazine.

With 554 passengers on board, he had enough ammunition to have killed and injured many people.

El Khazzani was known to French authorities and had been tagged with a *fiche 'S'*, the highest warning level for French state security. He was also similarly profiled by Belgian, German, and Spanish authorities. From 2007 to March 2014, it seems he lived in Madrid and Algeciras where he attracted the attention of Spain's authorities after making pro-jihad speeches and attending a known radical mosque, **he was also involved in drug trafficking.**

In addition to El Khazzani, two of his three accomplices were of **Moroccan** origin, Redouane El Amrani Ezzerrifi and Mohamed Bakkali, while another Bilal Chatra was Algerian.

Near Morocco's Rif Mountain cannabis growing region, on 3rd November 2015, the Spanish police arrested **three Moroccans** with strong ties to ISIS. It was later discovered their plan was to carry out attacks in Madrid at La Canada Real, a shanty town, and Vallecas, known as 'the rebel town of Madrid', a short walk from Atocha station the site of the 2004 terrorist attacks that killed 193 people - also by Moroccans who had links to drugs.

Paris, France, March 2016. A French national, Reda Kriket, was arrested in Paris with an "unprecedented" number of weapons and police believed was planning an act of "extreme violence". In his apartment, they found five assault rifles, seven handguns and the same type of explosive used in the attacks in Paris and Brussels in the recent past. Kriket had also been linked to the suspected ringleader of the Paris attacks.

In his flat in the Paris suburb of Argenteuil, they also found chemicals, false passports, brand-new mobile phones and two computers with information about bomb-making and jihadist groups. The arsenal included the TATP explosive used in the suicide bombs set off in Paris and Brussels by militants linked to Islamic State (ISIS). His arrest was during an operation just days after the attacks in Brussels.

Kriket was charged with participating in a terrorist group, possessing and transporting arms and explosives, and holding fake documents, the prosecutor said. Officials believe he had spent time in Syria in 2014 and 2015 and made several trips between France, Belgium and the Netherlands.

The following July, he was sentenced in absentia to 10 years in prison by a Belgian court for recruiting Islamist fighters for Syria. Investigations showed he had played a key financing role with money from robberies and stolen goods.

An associate, Abdelhamid Abaaoud, a Belgian of **Moroccan** origin, who was believed to have been the ringleader of the Paris attacks, was also absent for the trial.

In questioning by French investigators, Kriket said he was not a terrorist, but gave up little information. Three other men were held in suspicion of involvement in the same alleged plan. One was 32-year-old Frenchman Anis Bahri, who is believed to have travelled to Syria with Kriket. The other two have been identified as Algerian nationals Abderahmane Ameroud, 38, and Rabah M., 34. They have been charged in Belgium and will face a hearing on 7 April.

Reda Kriket

Abderahmane
Ameroud

Rotterdam, Netherlands: Two Moroccan-Dutch men were arrested in June 2018 for plotting a jihadist attack. The investigators found a video of the Erasmus Bridge in one of their cell phones. Two years later, they were sentenced to eight years in prison by a court in Rotterdam for planning an attack in the name of the Islamic State. One of the men was also convicted for destroying property in the prison while encouraged by the jihadist Mohamed Bouyeri, another Dutch Moroccan.

On 2nd November 2004 Bouyeri killed the Dutch film director, Theodoor van Gogh, in a terrorist attack simply because he objected to the content of his film, Submission. In it there was strong criticism of the treatment of women in Islam.

Arnhem, Netherlands: 8 October 2020 – Six men are jailed for up to 17 years for planning a major terrorist attack on a large event in the Netherlands and for setting up a terrorist organisation. Photos showing four of the group, known as the 27th September Cell, trying on bomb vests and waving Kalashnikov rifles while living in a house on a holiday park in Limburg were shown. Iraqi national Hardi N the ring leader was jailed for 17 years. Three others – Nabil B, Morat M and Wail el A – were jailed for 13. The remaining two, Shevan A and Nadim S, were jailed for 10.

Epilogue

Eulogio Paz

Terrorism has no justification, but it does need to be explained. The "understanding of the terrorist phenomenon" is necessary.

Although the international community has not yet adopted a general definition of terrorism, existing universal "sectoral" declarations, resolutions and treaties related to specific aspects of terrorism define certain basic acts and elements. In 1994, the General Assembly approved the Declaration on Measures to Eliminate International Terrorism in its resolution 49/60, in which paragraph 3 stated that terrorism includes "criminal acts for political purposes conceived or planned to provoke a state of terror in the population in in general, in a group of people or in specific people", and that such acts are "unjustifiable in all circumstances, whatever the political, philosophical, ideological, racial, ethnic, religious or any other type of considerations that are asserted for justify them» (OFFICE OF THE UNITED NATIONS HIGH COMMISSIONER FOR HUMAN RIGHTS "Human Rights, Terrorism and the Fight against Terrorism." Information Leaflet No. 32)

Thus, we have that, and throughout history, certain groups have used, and continue to use, terrorism to achieve objectives of independence, religious domination, racial supremacy, economic oppression, political power, in short. Nationalist terrorism, extreme left terrorism, extreme right terrorism and jihadist terrorism are the fundamental pillars of terrorism today.

Do terrorists kill for drugs, for money, for the mere pleasure of killing? No. There are political, economic or religious objectives, which may or may not be legitimate. For this reason, although a sexist crime may be more horrendous than a terrorist attack, we are not talking about "sexist terrorism". We can say the same in relation to any other type of crime that is not terrorism, be it drug trafficking or organized crime. The word terrorism is associated with the word "politics" and what makes terrorism illegitimate and condemnable is the way to resolve discrepancies; that is, killing the different, sowing terror among people and in society as a whole. The way to resolve conflicts must only be through democratic politics.

We are seeing different ways of resolving disagreements recently, for example, in Europe. Scotland (although Great Britain is no longer part of the European Union) is trying to resolve its desire for independence through democratic and political means; there is no ruling group that tries to resolve the situation through terrorism. Northern Ireland itself, which in the past suffered terrorist attacks by the IRA, today sees how its nationalist aspirations go through democratic endorsements and not through terrorist activity. The latest terrorist attack in Istanbul is indicative that there are those who continue to try to resolve potential conflicts through terror and not through political means.

Solving problems from a parliamentary seat is always preferable to the use of weapons and bombs. Dialogue and reaching agreements in the different forums that constitute a democratic society is the best antidote against terrorist violence.

Jihadism is today the most talked about form of terrorism, its ideology being the creation of the Caliphate, and the imposition of Sharia law, and using assassinations indiscriminately. Its leaders proclaim the violent Salafi doctrine as only correct one in Islam. However, its purposes should not be seen only from religious and ideological perspective. It is also necessary to know the political, al, economic, social or any other context in which they develop, the goal they what stimulates and motivates them, what makes them continue to have wers. Understanding the terrorist phenomenon is insufficient, it is eradicating calisation that is essential with regard to its prevention.

I say that hopefully tomorrow, better today! The jihadist terrorist anizations or any other existing terrorist group will issue a statement saying that y stop killing, as ETA did in Spain more than eleven years ago, since it had been feated by the rule of law. If Islamists, Christians, Jews or believers of any other eligion, ideological formulation or political ideology stop killing and commit to preaching their faith or ideology only through words, we will not be able to say that: "what they have not achieved by killing, they cannot They're going to get it now." In any case, to face "these faiths and ideas" there is the educational task (especially among youth), political work, awareness of the importance of a secular society in which everyone can be free to believe in whoever wants without society and the rule of law feel slaves of these "faiths and ideas."

Printed in Great Britain
by Amazon